A POWERFUL MINDSHIFT: GREATER VS LESSER

BY LADREW MURRELL

WWW.13THANDJOAN.COM

A Powerful Mindset Shift: Greater vs. Lesser. LaDrew Murrell. All rights reserved. No part of this publication may be reproduced, distributed, or transmitted in any form or by any means, including photocopying, recording, or other electronic or mechanical methods, without the prior written permission of the publisher, except in the case of brief quotations embodied in critical reviews and certain other noncommercial uses permitted by copyright law. For permission requests, write to the publisher, addressed "Attention: Permissions Coordinator," 500 N. Michigan Avenue, Suite #600, Chicago, IL 60611.

13th & Joan books may be purchased for educational, business or sales promotional use. For information, please email the Sales Department at sales@13thandjoan.com.

Printed in the U.S. A.
First Printing, June 2019
Library of Congress Cataloging-in-Publication
Data has been applied for.
ISBN: 978-1-7331313-3-9

DEDICATION

I dedicate this book to my mother, Opal Jean Murrell. My mother has been the most influential person in my life in the sense that she has displayed her spiritual strength and faithfulness through her daily words, actions, and interactions. She is the most disciplined and consistent person that I have ever known.

Without her, this book would never be written. Outside of the obvious, I had to be born. Opal Murrell has deposited in me the ability to know the Truth and accept it. Her constant pursuit of right-doing has made a way for many to see first hand the value of right-doing.

My dad, Larry Murrell, is a good man, a man that fits no stereotype. Today in America, absent fathers are prevalent, especially in the African-American culture. He defied these odds eleven times. My Dad has always been a provider and protector of his house by taking care of the physical needs of everyone that carries his name.

My brothers and I lived in fear of our dad; not meeting the expectation of a six-foot-four-inch man of steel was not the ideal way to have a successful day. Although he didn't tell us boys that he loved us, as a young boy, I remember my dad coming home from work and we would meet him at the door with a cheer, "Dad-dy's home" a hundred times. We would proceed to sit on his size fourteen shoe with our legs wrapped around his ankles as he would walk around the house. If you were not one of the first two that sat on his shoe, you would just climb onto his legs as if you were climbing a tree. Larry never let us down.

To my mother Opal, who believes in God, this is the answer to your prayers and the physical representation of the covenant between you and the Lord. May your house dwell in the presence of the Lord Jesus Christ our God forever. Amen.

This book was birthed from my lowest moment, when my understanding of this world and everything in it was challenged. If you have not experienced a circumstance that has made you question everything you have ever believed, this book will help you prepare for that time, as it comes to us all.

The beautiful thing about this book is that I began to write it as enlightenment showed itself in my life. At that time, I had just got fired from my head coaching position and needed to find a new school to teach and coach at. To make matters worse, I had no money to pay my bills or move. I lived off of the limit of my wife's credit card.

Then a crazy idea came to my mind: write a book! Although I have no formal qualification, I followed my heart.

I sold my twenty-two-inch rims off of my blacked out Dodge Charger on Facebook, took that money, and went to buy a computer. What was left over was given to my wife to repay debts that I had earned on the credit card.

I am now living out the book in real time as I have gone from: an unfaithful husband to a faithful husband, a good man to an honest, good man, a good dad to a father raising his sons with purpose and intent, fighting constantly with my ex-wife to co-parenting effectively, homeless to stable, unemployed to employed, a teacher to a business executive, a pornography addict to being free from use of it at all, abusing alcohol to not drinking at all, a victim to an entrepreneur. Just to name a few things.

I have written this book as a formula of success for those living under the difficulties that may be encountered in life. As this book was written for you, it was also written for me, so that I can hold myself accountable for staying on path with my life's purpose. I am working right alongside of you to become the ultimate version of myself, LaDrew Murrell.

ACKNOWLEDGMENTS

I would like to acknowledge a few very important persons in my life that have been my friends in times of need and continuously provide the inspiration for me to become my ultimate self. My sons LaDrew Jr. and Javion the Great. Many choices that I have made in my life will impact your life more so than it does mine. I will work twice as hard to influence you to do good in this world, as the consequences of my poor choices have left conditions and memories that are impossible to forget. LaDrew Jr.: You are full of compassion and empathy. This will be worth more than anything you work toward owning. Javion the Great: you are very similar to me, which means you could become of the conscious mind sooner than later. Boys, no father has ever had better sons. To my wife Hannah: My lady, no man has ever experienced the love that I have found in you. Everything changes; that is predictable. We have vowed to evolve together. Thank you for making that commitment to our marriage.

My siblings: Dionne, Laryee, Ainta, Larry Jr., Loren, Landon, Lindsey, Logan, Langston, Kennedy. My memories with all of you are held very close to my heart. I thank God that we have been chosen to be connected by bloodline. I love you all. My brother-in-law Byron and my sister in law Nikki. My best friend Saladean. Sal, you are the most loyal person that I have ever met. If I ever needed something and I could only call one person, it would be you; I'm not exactly sure if that is good or bad! My nieces: Brionna, Tamara Emorie, Morgan, Demi Vaughn, Lila, and Dajiah. My nephews: Byron Jr., Caleb, Christian, Isaiah, Jaxon, and Jordan.

To the many family friends that have been a blessing to myself and those I love. I could not dare to name just a few of you. There are many who have had an impact on the lives of the Murrell family. May you all experience the fullness of God's love and mercy that endures forever. Amen.

TABLE OF CONTENTS

The Outside of the Cup 11

Part 1
Chapter 1 Breaking Barriers 19
Chapter 2 Who and Why? 43
Chapter 3 Victim 79
Chapter 4 Overcome 103

Part 2
Chapter 5 Greater Versus Lesser 123
Chapter 6 What's at Stake 151
Chapter 7 Become the Solution 177
Chapter 8 Good - Better - Best 201

Part 3
Chapter 9 The Law You Should Know 217
Chapter 10 Worthwhile 239
Chapter 11 A Kingdom, Not Religion 257
Chapter 12 King of Kings 267

Final Thoughts 281
About the Author 285

THE OUTSIDE OF THE CUP

I have been in the public education field over the past decade in the roles of teaching and coaching. I have always taught in a Title 1 building, which means there is a "real world" dynamic within the building. There is a mixture of the "haves", which consists of your upper class that do not battle financial hardships. The middle class, are your blue-collar workers that earn everything by the hard work from their own hands. And the "have nots" live in poverty and eat free lunch. Through my observation, I have witnessed the need for an awakening by way of applied knowledge and mindshifts. That is the sole purpose of this content. To put the subconscious mind to the forefront of conscious thought is the objective we will pursue on this journey. I fit into this need also, as my world constantly has conflict in it. How we deal with conflict has everything to do with where we are in comparison to where we want to be. My lowest point resulted from divorce which disrupted every aspect of my life as I knew it, and affected my sons' and ex-spouse's lives all the more. This event significantly impacted my ability to parent my two sons, teach my curriculum, and coach extracurriculars. The people around me were getting the worst version of me that I had to offer the world. This caused me to think about the person I was giving the world. Is this my best self? As I noticed an unbalance within myself, I began to observe the adults in teaching and leadership roles. Upon reflection, it became obvious: we were all dealing with something. That consumed how we interacted with one another, which all stemmed from the conflict that we had inside ourselves and in our lives.

This led to my observations of our youth, their mindsets, and work ethic towards a higher purpose. My discoveries were enlightening as I found that we all suffer internally, daily. What is battled on the inside controls how we perceive and interact with the outside, leading us to connect with the outside to determine what to do next. We have become a reactive people, responding to what is given to us by life instead of demanding what we want out of it. The old saying revealed itself to me: "The blind lead the blind". From the least to the greatest, student and teacher alike, everyone battled to find answers to their *Whys*. I found that these statements resonate with us all:

- What is Truth?
- Who am I (Identity)?
- What is my purpose?
- How can I reach my dreams?
- How can I know the unknown?

I have heard stories from the worst lows to the greatest highs, but all things positive or negative faded and left only the memory. This memory would impact the present and the future, often interrupting our ability to move forward because we were either frightened by our past or content with our successes. There seemed to be one solution at the root of all uncertainties:

- Our soul holds our true identity. In this formless substance, it is the only place that we can find stability within ourselves that is unchanging. Simultaneously, our flesh and emotions seek what is ever changing to achieve comfort. The Great Conflict.

This contrast is the focal point in overcoming the most difficult circumstances in your life. It allows you to look through a lens that sees turbulence as a necessary attribute to acquire successful outcomes, because you realize that the war is between your soul and your flesh. Each one seeks to be first and will work every second of every day not to come in second place.

To develop the most sustainable version of ourselves, I offer this step-by-step guide to align your actions to the path of what you desire. I challenge you to evaluate your desires and where they come from. Is this desire from my soul, which is the part of me that is unchanging? Or, is this desire coming from my flesh, which is self-pleasing and seeks things that are constantly changing? This is important to recognize in order to prevent you from gaining things that are only temporarily satisfying, which will cause you to constantly chase after the next thing. But, if you are seeking what is formless through your formless soul, what is pursued is unchanging and available in quantities that are guaranteed to please those who seek it. So I ask you: Are you going through hardships, struggling to find truth, has your identity been lost, or are you wondering what your purpose is for this life? If so, this book is for you. I will coach you through the process of making your hardships fuel for your successes. No problem is too big, be it financial, divorce, abuse, depression, addiction, sexuality, anxiety, loss of loved ones, or identity uncertainty, just to name a few. The good news amongst the bad is that others have faced and overcome the obstacle you are facing. You must use this conflict to create a peaceful awakening in your life, otherwise the conflict will become magnified. This is what we want to avoid.

If you are reading this before your hardship has come, you will be well equipped to endure and overcome it when it shows up; and it will come sooner or later. If you are reading this during your troubles, it is a sign that the Formless Intelligence is working within you. If you have overcome great disadvantages in your life, you will be provided with a written formula that can be used to allow the conflict in your life to serve a positive purpose. No matter where you are in your journey, this book will help you find the narrow path leading to peace.

If your challenge is the result of self-inflicted choices or completely out of your control, you must find its identity. Once you have identified the mountain in front of you and where it came from, you must eliminate all things associated with its existence outside of yourself. Make a list of who you blame, accuse, hate, and envy for your troubles, so that you may refer back to this list to hold yourself accountable to not harbor hate or blame against these factors; it will only slow down growth, or eliminate the possibility of achieving your ultimate self altogether. Your list of things only distorts truth and blocks out light to prevent becoming your ultimate self because it makes you reactive to circumstances. Our goal is to be reflective and evaluate everything.

My objective through this body of work is to bring awareness to the barriers that lay between your current state and your ultimate self. The fact is that life is ongoing, so this process never stops, however, you are either moving closer to your ultimate self or further from it. Awareness of this does not make the journey any easier, but it does give you a fighting chance against what life allows to come your way. You cannot prepare for an enemy when you do not know who or what the opposition is. The one fact that is known is that everyone experiences hardships that take wisdom and perseverance to overcome. Therefore, seek wisdom as it informs your actions, and train to build stamina, because without it, you will fall at the hand of adversity.

We are all in this together. I am learning and growing daily through life's journey. I feel it is our duty to help each other along the way. We were all born with amazing qualities and gifts inside of us. Let's use our innate gifts to break through the barriers that are standing in the way of us being our ultimate selves.

PART 1

1

BREAKING BARRIERS

Lack of progress in our lives is totally connected to the inability to understand the purpose of the form and formless barriers in our lives.

-LaDrew Murrell-

When I was fourteen years old, my Dad, Larry Jr. (brother), and I were in a car accident. We were going southbound on the highway in the fast lane, which in the USA is the furthest lane to the left. As we were approaching a car in the middle lane of the three-lane highway, we entered its "blind spot", and at that time the car aggressively moved into the fast lane that we were in. The front passenger side of our car was hit. From the impact, we went crashing into the highway barrier at over sixty mph. The car then spun out in circles, eventually stopping horizontal to traffic in the middle lane. Thankfully, we were not hit by another vehicle. I remember us getting out of the car to check on one another. We found each other safe from harm, and I said, "Thank God for the barrier, because it prevented a head-on collision with northbound traffic." My father then asked if we were wearing our seatbelts. Neither Larry Jr. or I was. In the mid '90s, it was seen as uncool to wear seatbelts, especially if you were sitting in the front seat because it was easier to be seen by others in traffic. My father explained how the seatbelt is what keeps you from interacting with the outside world while in a car and how it acts as the barrier between you and danger. He also cursed the driver that hit our car and did not stop as they were the cause of the accident. Above the hit and run, my father was enraged at the driver's misuse of the dashed lines (lanes) on the highway that created invisible barriers between you and other vehicles traveling in the same direction. In that moment, I recognized the purpose and significance of barriers: seen and unseen.

A barrier can be defined as: 1) a fence or obstacle that prevents movement or access, or 2) a circumstance or obstacle that keeps people or things apart or prevents communication or progress. This puts into perspective how necessary some barriers are. For example, the walls of your home keep out intruders and protect you from weather conditions. You can also see how barriers work in preventing one thing from coming in contact with another by stopping progress. One of the most powerful barriers I have seen is the sand of the sea shore. It's amazing how it separates the vastness of the ocean from the land that we live on. Is there a barrier greater than this or more necessary?!

The process for a barrier to be broken is a task that must be intentional and strategic. We must understand and recognize that barriers come in all shapes and sizes, and some are not even visible. You will learn how to identify your formless barriers so that you can intentionally break those that are preventing you from progressing. You will also learn how to appropriately maneuver around the invisible barriers that keep you safe as you navigate through life with people to your right and left. Lack of progress in our lives is totally connected to the inability to understand the purpose of the formed and formless barriers in our lives.

A formless barrier is like the painted lines on a highway. They create invisible barriers that are to be acknowledged and respected. Knowledge of these barriers is what keeps everyone safe; lack of knowledge of these formless barriers puts you and others around you in great danger. Formless barriers are unique because every person's knowledge of them is at a different level due to their diverse life experiences. Their personal understanding changes how people apply their knowledge. This understanding can be influenced by race, socioeconomic status, religion, age, and culture.

A formed barrier can be seen with the eye. We are often reactive to these because our sense of sight informs us of its existence. If we like the barrier, we tend to use it to our benefit; and if we dislike, it we usually try to use force as a means of removing it. Our life experiences and values have an impact on whether we consider a barrier useful. For instance, police officers serve as physical barriers between right and wrong doing, but one's view of this barrier could be obstructed based on race, gender, class, culture, age, or circumstance. This realization is what makes this wonderful service a danger to those that serve in the capacity of law enforcement. Just like the formless barriers on the roads we drive on, the differences between us causes an inevitable gap in the interpretation of our view of police officers. This is what makes the barrier that stands as the defense of the law a risk to those who put on the uniform to honor their country.

Mutual Understanding

There are several terms that you will hear throughout this book, and I want to provide you with a reference to the vocabulary that is common within the text.

Formless

Things of this world are either form or formless. You cannot deny the presence of the air, although it is formless. We subconsciously breath it into our lungs, and we feel it every time we are in contact with nature. However, the air never takes on form because it cannot be contained by the form of anything; it is simply too vast. The emotions that we feel are also formless (not to be confused with action) as a result of formless energy. Abstracts that are formless by nature are extremely powerful. When barriers reside here, they are often difficult to identify because they become a part of our formless subconscious thought. What is formless cannot be seen or interpreted through sight, which immediately causes a barrier to form because of the dependence we have on our vision. Formless things are all of the ideas in your mind that have not evoked action. The Formless Law is this: What is formless can only remain this way for a little while, because formless energy manipulates form, which causes the corresponding action that follows.

An example of the formless: One man and one woman had an idea to get married and have children. The woman thought, "I will stay home and care for the children and prepare food for us daily." Without inspiration from cookbooks or TV shows, she made recipes from ideas or carried on traditions from her mother. The man thought, "I am a skilled worker with my hands. I will find work and be my own authority". Due to his one-of-a-kind skills, his work was of high demand, and he provided the income for his family. When married in 1970, the couple's once formless ideas took form. My ten siblings and I are the result of those ideas.

Formless Intelligence

What I will refer to as the Formless Intelligence is the cosmos and everything that keeps it aligned. At times, science can explain "it" but cannot naturally produce it. It provides the natural laws that we must respect. If we interrupt its natural state, we ourselves become subject to disaster. It is our intelligence that allows us to observe nature to find solutions and discover new ideas. We can see a parallel in how a hummingbird hovers over a flower and how this motion inspired the function of the helicopter.

Who makes sure that the sun comes up in the morning and the moon at night? Who makes the clouds stand poised and fill with rain in the harvest season? Who decides the beginning of the winter and spring equinox? We carry on and think very little about the essential things that allow us to exist because the Formless Intelligence is always at work.

Form

Form are the things in life that are physically present and ever-diminishing. Form can only disintegrate after it has been created. We are reminded of this when we look into the mirror or demand of our bodies that which we were once capable of in our youth.

Form encourages us to chase after it because of its fleeting sustainability. In this way it works to control us as we try to improve or acquire more form from the world: wealth, homes, cars, designer clothes, jewels, health, and the like. Form is always the result of our thoughts or someone else's thoughts. Everything you see is simply a thought that has manifested into form through time. All form corresponds to the thoughts of the people. To change the form that we see, we must change our thinking.

Two friends ride together to high school every day. One of them owns his prized possession: his dream car. This car earns him popularity and a status of superiority. He uses every dime earned by his hands to maintain his car. Meanwhile, the friend of the car owner invests in himself through his education. Time passes, and hey both graduate. Ten years later, they meet up to remember the old days, and the once popular friend pulls up in the same car covered with sun spots and a rusted spoiler. The other man owns a company and has assets worth millions of dollars, due to his formless investment.

Wisdom

The application of knowledge. To have knowledge and not apply it, or the inability to act on what is known, is the opposite of wisdom. To apply wisdom takes self-discipline, which supports the argument that self-government is the most essential element to one's progressiveness. You are only as wise as what you know and what you can act upon. Wisdom is the key element in defeating addiction because it removes the abuse of the stimulant one becomes addicted to. The harmful effects are known before it becomes an addiction, therefore the opposite of wisdom allows such a thing to take place.

For example, a person knows the harmful effects of tobacco because it is written boldly on the packaging. Wisdom allows a person the ability to never try this product, which gives them no chance to become addicted to it. The opposite of wisdom would be to know that the product is addictive and harmful to the body and still try it out.

Flesh

This term is like a chameleon as it connects with a person's ego, personality, emotions, physical attributes, and physical desires. Our flesh is the suit that we wear everyday, and it plays a large role in how we identify with ourselves as it is the form of a formless being. Its traits are very pronounced, which is how it works to dominate our identity. It uses what is seen and felt to connect the dots in our lives. The flesh is self-serving and disruptive. Our flesh competes to be first at everything, even if it kills us.

We may wish to quit something we are addicted to, but our flesh will not allow it; therefore the offense that is committed is not who we are but an aspect within ourselves that holds more power than our true identity. The power of the flesh allows the sensations it desires to dominate the thoughts of the mind. This part of who we are fights against the action we desire to take in bettering ourselves. We seek to use our time more wisely and do away with our unproductive habits, such as binge-watching TV shows. Our flesh is opposed to picking up a book, heading out to the gym, or taking the kids to the park. The flesh is asked to go outside of its comfort zone, and has a consistent response of, "No thank you." In order to deny our flesh, we must overrule it with our subconscious mind. The flesh seeks daily victories which creates a constant battle, like it or not.

Truth Barrier (Source) What is Truth?

What is perceived as truth has created barriers from the beginning of time. For every person's truth, someone else opposes that belief as false, which allows a form or formless barrier to evolve over time. The longer barriers remain, the stronger the barriers become, which makes them seem almost impossible to break. Truth barriers are so strong that wars have been waged, lives lost, sacrificed, and devoted based on what someone holds as true in their hearts. The fact is that truth in form always has and will be relative to the individual. This means there will always be barriers. Knowing this and applying this understanding is the first step in moving forward. Convictions are based on what a person believes to be true in their heart. These convictions become the motivation behind behavior, thoughts, and what a person spends their time on. What someone believes to be true has a large impact on his/her behavior which impacts all of us, our community, and our world. The answer is not that we coexist. This idea is impossible because some convictions put others lives in danger. Instead, we should understand the fundamental property of truth so that we can apply this knowledge in a way that is beneficial to everyone.

Truth in form can be debated, and the fact is that each stance may be valid, making both arguments true. In this sense, truth relies on an person's thought process, which has been influenced by many things, like a person's environment. Someone could make the argument that Michael Jordan is the best NBA player to have played the game, while the opposition may feel as though LeBron James is more deserving of that title. The two sides may never agree, making both athletes the greatest of all time depending on a person's perspective. While in another argument, these two players may not have even been in the discussion. In another example, a man is sitting in a restaurant with his wife who he believes to be the most beautiful woman in the room. Another couple sits three tables away, and the gentleman there holds the same belief about his wife. A religious man convicted in his beliefs worships his God or gods and works to convert a non-believer to his religion. Who is right? The fact is that as long is the truth is based on form, which is forever changing, there is no solid foundation for the truth when content and perspective are ever changing. In science, we learned that this is called a constant variable; without something being constant, there is no reliable means to understand a solution.

So how is the barrier broken when discussing truth in form? We are able to break this barrier, or navigate around it, by knowing that there is no truth in form. This idea allows everyone to hold their own belief system about what truth is when discussing truth that has no consistent means to it. This empowers you to enter a conversation with a wise mindset, because truth in form is based on opinion and must be defended. Therefore, hearing the values someone else holds in relation to form is simply their view which cannot be either right or wrong. This does not mean that you agree with them, however, in this sense all matters discussed get their due respect, keeping both individuals invested in the conversation. With mutual respect for others ideas, a constant is found that allows each person room to be reflective on his/her own beliefs in respect to a different perspective. Anyone can accomplish this and participate in growth conversations through conflicting ideas or perspectives. So the next time there is dialogue about religion or politics (which are matters made by man) consider these findings. Man-made systems that are created to solve man-made problems must be looked at under the lens of form, which is why laws change and religions have multiple denominations within a single sect. Laws change and religious practices evolve over time, but what is true has been since the beginning of time and will remain that way. This is the truth of the Formless Intelligence.

    Formless barriers are not as simple to understand because they are interpreted through our five senses after they have taken on form. Our higher selves activate this realm where love, compassion, fear, faith, anger, and many other formless sensory abstracts reside. These senses in the formless matter often turn into actions producing form, which immediately take them out of the formless realm and can no longer be seen in this unchanging light. It must remain formless to hold its truth. We all know what love feels like, but when it is expressed in form, its truth becomes distorted and reliant on opinion or perspective. Tough love shown from a father may look completely different than the nurturing love shown from a mother, but both are expressions of love. The existence of love is truth; love is today what it was two thousand years ago. The self-development that differentiates how this truth is expressed in form is the beauty of human evolution. Jesus Christ is a great example. The Bible explained how he used a formless truth to guide his motives and actions which ultimately changed the world in a way that has been unparalleled.

It is important to understand that there is a formless truth that is unchanging. The Formless Intelligence is incomprehensible by the human mind. The acknowledgement of this brings wisdom and with it, a solution within itself. We are all depending on the Formless Intelligence as much as we depend on the oxygen we are breathing in now. The oxygen taken in provides life to individuals who will commit very different acts. Meanwhile, the air remains the same. If the truth is formless and produces life and sustains life, the form that takes place due to truth should be recognized in ALL life and the sustainability of it. This means that everything we see is important, even if we disagree with it. Opposing thoughts place us in a seat of judgement where we have no right to be seated. This is true unless we hold the title of a judge by your government or kingdom, but being given authority to judge does not make your judgement the truth. Just look at the many different judgements on abortion across the world today.

To break the truth barrier is to understand that only one truth exists, and it is (and will remain) formless. It is the Formless Intelligence that keeps the night separate from the day, the seas separate from the land, and seasons consistent with the time. Anything that takes form becomes relative truth and must be respected as such. I understand that this is a difficult finding to accept, but having an open mind to explore this will vastly increase your likelihood of grasping this concept. Allow natural disasters to help you understand this teaching. We have no control over them happening, we just hope that they do not come. But when they do, there is absolutely nothing we can do to prevent it. Our mindshifts to hope, another formless abstract, to survive it.

Mismanagement, or lack of understanding of the truth barrier, is what dissolves marriages, creates financial problems, starts wars, or endangers public places of congregation. This barrier can only be non-combative if people are educated beyond their race, socioeconomic status, religion, gender, democratic affiliations, and cultural beliefs. Neglecting this barrier by lack of investment in yourself will force us to operate unsuccessfully in life because these types of barriers are present, whether we are aware of it or not. Mismanagement of this barrier gives us a false sense of power that we, or the next generation, will have to repair. For example, any man and woman have the power to make a child, but it does not mean that they should. This happens all of the time, which results in a layered society (with poverty being one of the worst layers).

Lack of understanding of the truth barrier causes people to make judgements or commitments prematurely. Failing marriages, personal debt, and absent parents are evidence of this effective use and misuse of the truth barrier.

You break the **truth barrier** with **Source.** The source is where the truth lies, and everything has a source. If something is man-made, it also has a source, which is biased to the maker. A fish must be connected to water; the water is its source. This truth cannot be argued because it connects to the source of the fish, and if you put the fish anywhere except in water, it will die. A lion must be connected to the land; the land is its source. This truth cannot be argued because it connects to the source. If you put the lion anywhere but on land in the proper region, it will die. You yourself are essentially star dust. As the stars, cosmos, earth, and everything in it are connected to the Formless Intelligence as its source, so are you.

Something created by human hands or thoughts also has a source, however, it is subject to the creator or manufacturer's beliefs. This is why we disagree as to what we hold as truth in things that are man-made. The source of something man-made was selected by the man that made it, meaning we have the right to agree or disagree with it. In these things, we are usually given options so that we can choose our source.

Think about what you have chosen for your religion, political affiliation, car brand, education (public or private), or phone provider. We have options in all of these areas because they are man-made. We will only connect with something if we agree with its source when we deal with man-made things. When dealing with man-made source, we must enter this with the understanding that we often will not see eye to eye in these matters. This empowers us to have the ability to enter a situation knowing that the conclusion may end with disagreement. The application of this knowledge comes when we do not judge another person's truth that is connected to a man-made source. Instead, we hear their views and, in turn, they can hear our views. This is why being convicted in a man-made source is extremely dangerous. People will be divided this way and possibly convicted in a way that they eliminate anyone with opposing beliefs. This can happen because there is nothing constant in man-made truth. Think about your religion and how its beliefs and practices have evolved over time. If you believe in no higher power at all, think about the behaviors linked to that belief and how those behaviors have also evolved over time.

Our day is governed by two lights, the sun which governs the day and the moon which governs the night. They share this responsibility, and science works to explain this phenomenon. However, science cannot produce or alter this work. Its source is outside of man's hands, just as your source is outside of man's hands. Again, I will say you are connected to the same source as the cosmos. This is the understanding of source, a source that we have no control over and cannot deny that we are connected to. This source is connected to the Formless Intelligence, and in this source, we can simply put our hope. We count on oxygen being available to us, but have no control over whether it comes or goes. The truth is that man does not control the coming up or going down of either of these two great lights, although science can explain this phenomena. Science has also mastered cloning, but cannot put a soul into the artificial life it creates.

Arguing the source that controls these things is not the purpose of this content, but the understanding of truth is. We can now define truth as the source in which a thing is created and must remain connected to in order to function.

- The truth barrier must be broken because where truth is in form differs from person to person. And where there is no truth, there is no common progress.

I must state that humans are able to deny the reality of the source that governs our lives. Consider the fish mentioned earlier. While it is in the sea, it could deny that it is in the sea or that it even needs the sea to exist. When problems arise, fish could curse the sea and blame it for its adversities. Still, the fish is connected to its source. The fish could even create a "bubble" to put itself into while in the sea as a safety mechanism to protect it from all of the stress that comes with living in the sea. However, as long as it is connected to the sea, at any time the fish could swim out of the bubble and into the sea of endless possibilities. This same fish could be caught and put into a large aquarium, safe from predators and fed on schedule, providing quite a comfortable and non-threatening living environment. However, unconnected to its natural source, it can never reach or grow to its full potential; although life in this realm may seem very satisfying. The aquarium minimizes what the fish could be, compared to being connected with its natural source. Any offspring born into this reality may never know that the sea exists, and their truth will be impacted by this unnatural environment. The offspring are born into a disadvantage that almost cripples its chances of becoming whole, only because the offspring is unaware that its true source is outside of the false environment it was born into.

- The fish in the sea has unlimited resources to find its identity and purpose because it is connected to its source. This is us, and though we may complain and gripe about life, as long as we are connected to the Formless Intelligence, we have Hope. Here, unlimited resources of form and formless are available to ALL. Even if you deny the source or put yourself into the "bubble" to protect yourself, at any moment you could remove those restraints from your mind and live. Here, oneness is possible. (3/3rds whole).
- The fish in the aquarium that is safe from predators can never live in its purpose or find true success. This is a person with wealth in form, with enough money to buy anything their heart desires. This person believes that their source is

from man-made things because that is how they acquired the things they have gained. Here, you cannot possess true Love, Faith, or Compassion, Hope, and all of the formless abstracts that connects us to the Formless Intelligence, because you can only possess what has been made by man. Here, you can only become a fraction of who you are because you are not connected to the source. (2/3^{rds} maximum).

- The fish born into the aquarium adopts a false environment for its truth. This is also like a child born into poverty, or extreme wealth. The offspring are born into a disadvantage that almost cripples its chances of becoming whole, only because the offspring is unaware that its true source is outside of the false environment it was born into. The environment that lacks form or has the resources to acquire anything of form that could be named. In both situations, the ability to become connected with the natural source is most certainly difficult when placed in a false environment, but it is not impossible. One may catch a glimpse of another realm, but it is snatched away by the conditions within their environment. This creates barriers, leaving each dimension (Soul, Mind, and Body) in conflict with the other all the time. Here, you are one dimensional and incapable of operating on more than one dimension at a time. (1/3rd fraction of self)

Truth can only be found in its formless state because, in this realm, there is unchanging consistency. We are able to understand truth by connecting it to its source. Is the source of a discussion man-made? If so, there is no such thing as truth. Truth in form is always relative to the individual that holds that truth. Truth in form must also be defended by the persons who hold that as truth in their hearts. Formless truth is unimpacted by mankind because its source is the Formless Intelligence. This truth is unchanging and reliable due to its connectedness to the Formless Intelligence and its ability to remain formless.

Can any truth in form be proven as fact? Can any truth in form stay the same? No, truth in form must evolve over time. This evolution adapts to the changes and needs of the human culture that holds that truth. What then is reliable and unchanging? That which is not controlled or manipulated by mankind! Formless abstracts never change or alter its ways. Due to its complexity, it can remain formless and connect itself to the Formless Intelligence, so that its purpose will not be compromised. To find truth, you must find the source of the thing you are seeking truth of.

CHAPTER 1
SUMMARY

There are barriers that lie between us and the things that we desire in life. These barriers prevent us from living the life that we dream of. Some of the barriers are formless. This means that they cannot be seen with the eye. A common formless barrier that we all have encountered is fear. Fear is one of the most successful formless barriers that prevents one from reaching their ultimate self. When a barrier is formless, we must become familiar with it so that we can learn how to navigate around what is not necessary. Each living person understands formless barriers at different levels. This leaves room for error when we try to collaborate on a common vision. Everyone plans a safe commute, however, another person's understanding and use of formless barriers may cause you to get into an accident.

As we proceed, you must understand formless barriers like time. Time inevitably places a formless barrier between us and our ability to understand. However, knowledge and understanding allows one the ability to apply wisdom regardless of time. This application of knowledge (which is every action of every day) is what produces what we see in form. Form, being tangible, is much easier for us to understand because it allows our senses to interpret for us. When things of form are seen or heard repeatedly, they become programmed in the subconscious mind and recreated by the individual that saw it. Evidence of this would be a toddler taking on the same mannerisms and phrases as their parents.

The Formless Intelligence is the wisdom that aligns the universe by strategic planning. It allows everything to function according to its will so that we may have our own free will. Regardless of what we choose to do, the Formless Intelligence waits patiently for us to adopt its wisdom and apply it to our lives. This formless presence is the great mystery that everyone seeks relationship with through religion or science so that solace may follow and triumph over fear.

Your form is your flesh, and our form is what unites us to one another. Our flesh is what we battle against each day as we strive to become what we are meant to be. If you are not aware of the desires of your flesh as you go about your day, it will rule over you and cause only destruction, as it seeks only easy victories and self satisfaction. Flesh unconnected to its source is ruthless, unorderly, and predictable.

This brings us to Source. If you find the source of a thing, you will find the truth. To find the truth about yourself, you must find your source and tap into it. Things are not self sustaining; they must have a source, and only the source can solve and fix issues of what it created. This means that a psychiatrist cannot fix another human because they are not the source of that person. It also means that children will stray away from the ways their parents taught them, and parents will be short of answers because parents are not the source of their children; they are the means in which the child was conceived.

Understanding truth is a process. And in this journey, you will acquire the tools needed to understand Truth completely. First you must learn how to find truth through the source of a thing.

2

WHO AND WHY?

"You will never find yourself if you do not take the time to get to know who you are."

-LaDrew Murrell-

Identity Barrier (Truth Applied + Time) Who am I?

Your identity is made up of three aspects within yourself:

1. **Soul** - Connected to the Formless Intelligence. Provides instincts, consciousness, and holds your true identity/purpose. What is inside of you is unlimited.
2. **Mind** - There are two parts to the mind: Subconscious, and Conscious. The Subconscious mind is the mediator and

power center that allows your life to mirror your thoughts and has the power to make anything possible. The Conscious mind is connected to your senses and reacts to what it receives from your senses. It is far less powerful than the subconscious mind because it works off of form.

3. **Body** - Your senses and how you interact with the physical world. What you take in feeds the conscious mind. This has everything to do with who you are and how you look. What your body can do for you impacts how you feel about yourself.

The identity barrier prevents oneness with self as the Soul/Mind/Body oppose one another, causing lack of cohesiveness. This results in turmoil on the inside as you are at war with yourself, and then it reflects this on the outside. Most often, we are not aware that this is happening, which is why most cases people's lives are not what they wished they were. You are currently operating in one of the following realms within your Identity:

- 1/3 or 33.3 percent by identifying with one area. The fish born into the false reality.
- 2/3 or 66.6 percent by identifying with two areas. The fish that lives in the aquarium.
- 3/3 or 100 percent by identifying with all three areas. Only available within the realm of the Source.

- The ultimate self operates as One.

If you are not One, and operating as your ultimate self, you are much more likely to become intercepted by the foul abstracts of life. These troubles link to your identity in place of your true self: addiction, divorce, mental illness, materialism, dishonesty, and the like. This is because your senses are the primary connection to you and the world, allowing you to invest most in the form that pleases the flesh. Think about someone born into poverty. How easy would it be for them to fail school and steal from someone that has something they want or need? Then again, think of how unlikely the same would be with someone raised in a nurturing environment connected to their source. Without financial lack, this thought would not likely enter the conscious mind nor be acted upon. Now, think about someone born into extreme wealth where every fix could be bought. How easy would it be for them to depend on medicine, alcohol, tobacco, or illegal drugs to cope with the issues of life? Then again, think of how unlikely the same would be with someone that understands their connection to the Formless Intelligence. They are doubtfully even entertained with the same thoughts of coping, because of their understanding of identity and connection to source.

Identity is based off of what you perceive as truth. If what you believe to be truth is in form, your identity will forever change, and you must defend yourself by your beliefs and feelings. The identity barrier works like this: There were two students that attended the same school from grade school until their current placement in middle school. They were never best friends, and they never hung out outside of school, but they had seen each other develop since kindergarten. The first student was a girl, and she loved playing with the boys. She was even referred to as a tomboy all her life. She fit in with the guys more so than with the girls and played coed sports for the majority of her youth. Her parents were wealthy and held jobs that required extensive travel time. As she grew, her body began to take the form of a lady, but she felt as though she identified with a feeling of masculinity from within. So she began to transition into a male. The second student was from a hard working middle class family. The young man's dad used to be a professional soccer player in Mexico. All of his life he wanted to be like his father, so he pursued soccer all year round. His parents worked multiple jobs in order to pay for his team fees so that he might make a name for himself. Approaching his eighth grade year, he had made the top recruiters list among young athletes. He returned back to school after summer break and approached his classmates with a bad limp and missing his right arm from the elbow down. His face was downcast. The third student was a transfer student that had been homeschooled until the eighth grade. He quickly became an outcast. He came to school everyday with a packed lunch and the same outfit on. Well his shirt would change, so he only wore the same shirt every other day. He always wore this jean jacket with fur on the collar, with white High Top Converse All Stars. Despite him not fitting in, he was an excellent musician. He always wore headphones in his ears and played the air drums to whatever song he was listening to. He never seemed to be phased by anything.

It came time to graduate high school, and out of the three students, only one was left. The student that transitioned in middle school changed her mind and did not go through with becoming a male. She matured into a very pretty young lady, but she transferred due to the embarrassment of her past identity. No one knew where her and her family moved. The student that had been homeschooled ended up taking his life by overdosing on his parents prescription pain pills. No note was left, and no one could seem to figure out why. This happened during winter break of his sophomore year. The second student that lost his arm and damaged his femur graduated as valedictorian. He also started a large non-profit organization in his community. He became passionate about getting artificial limbs to those who could not afford them so that they would not be limited from fulfilling their life's purpose.

The result of identifying yourself through a "thing" is that you become vulnerable. This is because the "thing" linked to your identity could drastically change any moment, and is changing day by day. If unexpected changes occur, it leaves you without an identity, and you become lost in the world until a new identity is found. A person without purpose or identity becomes a danger to themselves and the society they live in. Their new identity, if found in form, will always be compared to their identity of the past and their new motives will revolve around keeping their new identity. This puts all other affairs on the back burner. When someone struggles with their own identity, all relationships in their life suffer. This struggle impacts their behavior due to the fact that their existence is completely reactive in this state. Therefore, they are a danger to themselves and their society because unethical behavior will always serve as a quicker means to obtaining what the reactive flesh desires to have. If a person feels that their identity has been taken from them or is not accepted, they feel as though they have nothing to lose, which puts many lives at risk. Relationships suffer because you can only offer the world a percentage of who you are, which is not the ultimate self–it is actually in contrast with everything your true identity strives to be. Here, you cannot relate to yourself because you are a false sense of yourself. And it is impossible to relate to others in a organic way because you are not your true self. Teen suicide rates in America is strong evidence of this prevalent issue.

    Your **Source** is formless, and you must connect to this source in order to have an identity that does not change. If we are not connected to our source, we cannot live in full measure. When connected to this source, we become affiliated and related to the universe so that the Formless Intelligence is working within us. Acceptance from others simply cannot compete with the importance of self-acceptance. In the light of oneness, our being does not have to bounce from one place to another; instead, it can remain steady due to its unchanging source. As you know, a fish can live inside of a bubble in the sea. In this case, a person has chosen to disconnect from the source, meaning they cannot live in full measure compared to what they are capable of. If you are not connected to your Source, you are minimized and incapable of being or feeling complete. A fish connected to its source in the ocean is unlimited in its capabilities and has its true identity available to it. If you live unconnected to the Formless Intelligence, you are the fish rich in poverty, wealth, or any other man-made source of sustaining life. When you become connected to the Formless source, you become like the fish in the ocean—your potential is available to you. Most often, one does not realize what realm they are in unless they are intentionally connected to the Source. Remember one may be connected to the source but develop a shelter around themselves, such as the fish inside of the sea that lives in inside the bubble. All realms are available to us; the choice is completely up to you. What you choose will impact your identity.

A person must know themselves in order to have successful relationships with others. This identity crisis contributes to the percentage of failing marriages. The absence of fathers in their children's lives are also a root problem, creating strong barriers that stem from lack of identity. When your identity is in form, this barrier separates you from who you really are, leaving you subject to circumstances that constantly change. Evidence supports this as the misunderstanding of identity was the factor that led my first marriage into divorce. In my coaching experiences, I have taken on the role of a father figure to my athletes, as many coaches do. Absent parents control what a child sees in their upbringing. Noticing that something is absent, something else is pursued in order to fill that void. This creates no other means than to acquire a false sense of identity.

In the public school setting, I observed students at all levels (K-12) battling with identity issues. Depending on who a student was with, where their location was (classroom, electives, conferences, extracurricular activity, or at a grocery store with parents) their identity would change. In some instances, I saw students put on five different personas throughout the course of one day. Outside of my observations, their identity could have changed more times. As circumstances or location changed, so did their identity. This created a huge problem because they were always chasing who they thought they were supposed to be depending on where they were and who they were with. As students got older, this barrier became stronger and more difficult to break because it had become a normal way of life. I have seen behavior contracts and positive reinforcement strategies used to promote desired recurring behaviors, but this only made matters worse by creating another persona for the student to take on. Students would change their behavior to earn a certain reward but afterward, their freedom was earned through compliance to behavioral strategies used against them.

The identity barrier cannot be broken with the foundation built on form. Coaching at the high school level, I saw these behavioral strategies in a more evolved light. Students would earn grades that deemed them eligible for participation, and for some, this was their only motivation to pass the standard five-class minimum because their identity lied within the extra-curricular activity. I have seen students fail to receive a scholarship continue to perform within what they saw as their identity and, in turn, becoming non-productive members of their community, which increases the risk of undesired acts occurring within the community. Teen crime rates and teen pregnancy are just a few examples of the power and effectiveness caused by the identity barrier.

Grades also contribute to the identity crisis because students fight so hard to earn a letter that they feel will identify them as sufficient or not. A student earning all A's gets praise and recognition for the letter that identifies them. Meanwhile, a student rich in non-measurable abstracts such as love, compassion, empathy, humor, integrity, faith, courage, perseverance, and collaboration gets overlooked because their grade point average is a 2.0 on a 4.0 scale. We have failed miserably in an attempt to assess and empower our youth.

I also observed educators struggling with this same issue. Teachers and coaches viewed their job title as who they are, and when a leader was hired, I watched their behavior patterns conform to the stereotype provided by the title they held. Educators would even identify one another based off of the title they held, which created barriers between departments and contributed to the lack of staff cohesiveness. This identity barrier affects all relationships and shapes its society. Formless barriers were created by the hierarchy educators make according to the content areas in which they taught. For example, an English department may feel that their content area is more important than the art teachers job. The English teachers become upset that both receive the same pay, and one department despises the other.

Knowing this provides us with the consistency that it was to be understood; almost everyone's identity changes as they go from place to place, leaving no consistent behavior patterns for us to be identified by. Therefore, teachers were viewed in a different light by students. A particular teacher was held in high regard by one student and hated by another, and a particular student was enjoyed by a one teacher and disliked by another. This system is a recipe for chaos.

The barrier of truth also disrupts our progress because we identify one another according to outward things that are changing. A child is identified as one who should listen, take orders, and not object to adults. Adults charge other adults to think similarly because we should have all learned important values and morals as a child. Any system divided against itself cannot succeed, and lack of identity leads to division. If everyone identified with the Source that we are connected to, an awakening of oneness would occur within ourselves and the world. In the reverse, identifying with things puts us all on different plains. This is why identifying yourself or others by race, religion, culture, academic performance, athletic ability, looks, or income leads to a dead end road.

Think of the natural world that we live in and how nature does not allow itself to have these identity issues. Instead, it fulfills its purpose and does not compete with other natural resources. This creates a oneness due to nature's connection with the Formless Intelligence. Take precipitation for example: the rain does not try to do the sun's job. It simply rains on the earth and supplies fresh water for our ecosystem, never getting confused in its purpose, because it knows its identity. Thankfully, the natural world works this way and does not take after the inconsistencies of mankind.

To break this barrier, we must realize that our true identity is formless. We are not our job title, outward appearance, age, or cultural stereotype. We are not our assets and finances because our gift cannot be found in them, although our gift may allow us to acquire these things. Identity evolves, but it does not change based on what car you drive, how many friends you have, or how big your house is. Your identity can only be found if your mind is free from the bondage of your flesh. You are an intrinsic being that seeks to live for a higher cause. Your purpose is found through passion in the work you create, which comes from your true identity. In this manner, no matter what you have, where you are, who you are with, or what you are doing, your identity does not have to change.

This is the big answer to the common question: **Who am I?** You are a formless being with a job for the purpose of temporarily assisting you as you are finding or developing your true gift: what you were born to do. Your job is not what you were born to do. When you are working within your gift, it is no longer called your job. You rename it, because you are working within **your purpose**. The craft of your purpose may take a while to evolve, which is why it is necessary to have a job; your unfulfilling job becomes a bit more bearable each day knowing that there is a greater purpose for you. Our job finances our life until our gift is developed.

If you are working as a student or in a career that you know is not fulfilling your purpose, understand that it is necessary for you to be there in order for you to find your purpose. Once you find your identity (which is where purpose resides) it must be given time to mature. Your job, even if you dislike it, is a necessary step in the process of you developing your ultimate self.

- The identity barrier must be broken because, without your identity you, will always be chasing after "something". Even if you catch it, it will forever change because it is form, only leaving you the option to continue to chase after it. Where there is no identity, there is no true purpose.

Take this time to write down all the different personas you take on based off of who you are with, where you are, or what you are doing (see Figure 1). Are you a different person when you are: parenting, at your job, out with friends, at your parents house, at school, at home, or with your spouse? If you behave differently in these dynamics, you are having identity conflicts with the outside world and may be experiencing an unclear identification of self. This is why we ask the question: **Who am I?**

If you have this question, the identity barrier is a stumbling block for you. And as long as you are connecting your identity to form, the only option is for your false identity to run away from you, causing you to stumble with this global question.

You break the identity barrier with **time**. You will never find yourself if you never take the time to get to know who you are. Think about how you spend your time, especially your down time. Technology and the business of life work against you in this matter. It is important that you make a weekly schedule that maximizes how productive you can be. You must have **self-discipline** to hold yourself accountable to this schedule. Two and a half hours everyday should be connected with self-development. This is a **minimum** requirement in order to answer the question: Who am I? You must use the time that you are given very intentionally to find the answers you are seeking. Your Identity is found through your formless self, which is connected to the Formless

Intelligence. Without this source you could not live, function, or be.

Figure 1 (Fill in the blank boxes)

Who You Are Surrounded By	What is Your Environment?	Behavior Patterns	Description of This Identity
Spouse/Significant Other	Car/Commute		
Children/Siblings	At home		
Coworkers	On the job		
Best Friends/Night Life	Most common hangout location		
Alone	At home		

What you are currently spending your time on shows you where your priorities lie. If you have not made yourself a priority in your own life, you are not as effective as you could be. You may justify your actions and say that you are providing for your family and you don't have time for a schedule, or that it is not realistic for your lifestyle due to hardships, but think of the person you are giving to the world. Is it the ultimate you? If it is not, you are doing everyone in your sphere of influence a disservice. If you are not taking intentional time out of each day to become complete, you are putting a fraction of yourself into the tasks you are doing: being a spouse, parent, employee, employer, sibling, son/daughter, and the like. All of these roles suffer due to lack of investment in self, and lack of oneness. So it is not selfish or irresponsible to take proper care of yourself through the use of your time, which costs you nothing. Everyone has different responsibilities based on age, environment, marital status, dependents, along with other factors. However, everyone is given 24 hours each day. Here is an example of a week that would develop the ultimate self through proper use of time

Weekly Schedule Example

	Monday	Tuesday	Wednesday	Thursday	Friday
6:00 -6:45 a.m.	Reading & Meditation				
6:45 -7:30am	Prepare for The Day				
7:30 -8:00 a.m.	Commute: Audio Book	Commute: Motivational Speech	Commute: Classical Music	Commute: (Aloud) Affirmations & Visualization	Commute: (Aloud) Gratitude
8:00 a.m. – 12:00 p.m.	Job Title				
12:00 – 1:00 p.m.	Lunch & Read	Lunch & Socialize	Lunch & Workout	Lunch & Social Media	Lunch & Read
1:00 – 5:00 p.m.	Job Title				
5:00 – 7:00 p.m.	Active Parenting or Self Fulfillment	Kids Extracurricular & Workout	Active Parenting or Self Fulfillment	Kids Extracurricular & Workout	Active Parenting or Self Fulfillment
7:00 – 9:00 p.m.	Relationship Building & Dinner	Relationship Building & Dinner	Relationship Building & Dinner	Relationship Building & Dinner	Relationship Building & Dinner

9:00 – 9:40 p.m.-	Relationship Building with Spouse	Favorite Hobby	Relationship Building with Spouse	Favorite Hobby	Relationship Building with Spouse
9:40 – 10:00 p.m.	Read, Meditate, or Pray					
10:00 pm.	Sleep					

	Saturday	Sunday
6:00 – 7:30 a.m.	Read with Tea or Coffee	
7:30 – 8:00 a.m.	Visualize Goals, Meditate, Pray, or Gratitudes	
8:00 – 9:00 a.m.	Fasted Workout	

- If your identity is a stumbling block for you, use your time to in order to find who you truly are, and your purpose will be revealed.

The schedule makes specific time to develop the soul, mind, and body. You will learn that society and technology has trained you in a way that makes it difficult to spend time with yourself because we have become dependent on other people's opinions or having our cell phones in our hands. However your soul, mind, and body are all necessary components in the proper functioning of the ultimate self. If one area is weak, it negatively impacts the other areas or puts it into conflict with the other areas. The goal is to become conscious about what you are spending your time on that impacts your ability to make the soul, mind, and body operate as one unit.

Each of these aspects (soul, mind, and body) may have layers of barriers between them, causing your identity to remain a stumbling block. The use of your time must become a priority to develop these areas in a way that brings consciousness. The subconscious mind allows you to immediately know when stimuli is presented to your soul.

The conscious mind alerts you when your senses provides you with information from the outside world. Both elements should be involved in coming up with a response to any and everything. These elements are listed in order of importance. Your identity cannot be your body because it is form, which means it is changing every day, making it impossible to identify with. However, many people try to identify with their body because it is what everyone (including themselves) can see, so they alter it in any way they feel will gain them acceptance. No one is above this, however, we must be aware of this battle. Your height, looks, and body type are the means you can use to accomplish your purpose. You prioritize your health in order to operate at a high level physically.

Your mind is the mediator between your soul and your body and will always conform to the most dominant presence. This makes your mind a receiver, which takes in info and then can put it out after the information is translated. Your mind translates info into things like fear, doubt, confidence, love, faith, and opportunity, depending on the person. This is why your soul must be the focal point of your identity, and the majority of your time should be spent on strengthening the bond between the soul and mind. This will allow the body to act accordingly and the mind to operate on higher frequencies. This is where thoughts become things, from the power of manipulation of the invisible world.

Becoming one is a work in progress that must be focused on daily. You must exercise this practice continually because you could lose it at a moment in time. Being one today does not mean that you will be tomorrow. And if you are not one today, that does not mean that you will not be tomorrow. You must work daily in order to attain this and keep it. One can never truly say, "I have arrived," because we are always evolving.

Once your identity has been found, you will notice a self-acceptance that was not present before, and your soul will guide your emotions. You will stop comparing yourself to others, and fulfillment will no longer be found in materialism, opinions of other people, or what you look like. The way you respond to things will change because you are not connected to form as you were before; you are connected to the Formless Intelligence. This is the goal of breaking the identity barrier. Use your time wisely.

Relationship Barrier
(Truth & Identity Applied)

Now that we understand truth and have found where to locate our identity, we can now focus on relationships, and the barriers within them. If you are not consciously applying the knowledge gained from understanding truth and your identity, having effective relationships is not possible. You will only keep the relationships in your family that can not go away due to blood line. Barriers within relationships are what causes the partnership not to work in full capacity, and a barrier in one relationship multiplies itself by infecting other relationships in the same person's life. If you have not mastered oneness, you cannot give someone your complete self. If you are not one and you are married, your marriage cannot be whole. If you are not one, your friendships have an artificial foundation, and when tested by life, the relationship will not last. The barrier is strengthened when its existence is never recognized; lack of knowledge destroys the ability to overcome. Breaking this barrier comes from opening up this conversation to your family, spouse, or your friends so that you may use one another to see more clearly in the journey of becoming one.

A relationship barrier is like a spouse struggling to love because the identity of their partner has changed in their eyes. When they married, one honored the other because of their life-long academic success and wealthy family background. They lived comfortably without the threat of poverty, like the fish in the aquarium. They were abundant only in the matters of the measurables in life: degrees, grades, money, and career. What lacked was oneness created from connection to source. Living in the two dimensional realm, this connection was not possible. Eventually, one spouse lusts after a more stimulating relationship where the matters of identity are new, and the marriage dissolves. Not knowing the marriage was built on a foundation that could not weather the storm, the divorce was a surprise to family and friends, while this is the only acceptable ending to such a circumstance.

This barrier is broken when the knowledge of **Truth** and **Identity** are applied. Failure to apply knowledge of these formless barriers cause many troubles: failed marriages, parenting issues, sibling rivalries, failing governments, unstable friendships, dating issues, and lack of oneness within yourself. As you think of the relationships in your life that are not functioning at an optimal level, think of how you are applying the understanding you have of truth and identification of self. These are guaranteed to be at the root of the problems that you face in your relationships.

If a person is convicted in what they believe to be true, it allows them to lead by example. This provides a consistent place for the relationship to fall back on. My mother is a Christian, and her convictions are so strong that it caused me and many of my siblings to disagree with her for the majority of our lives. When we were inconsistent growing up, she remained the same, and leading by example made her stance even stronger. My mother was the only person in the relationship that was operating on all three dimensions consistently. In high school she would tell us not to drink, smoke, or do drugs. Although we may have rebelled, our mother has never been seen drinking, smoking, or doing drugs to this day. She would tell us to be careful about what we would watch on TV, or be careful about the music we would listen to. And although we may have rebelled, we never saw her watching or listening to something that did not align with her beliefs. Even though we didn't recognize it at the time, the oneness within her subliminally showed itself since our childhood. She is still the same today. Her oneness allows her spouse and children to have a relationship that operates on a high frequency. If you do not agree with her convictions, or even if you yourself are not one, the relationship has a chance because one person is whole. I have seen her friends come and go; the friends that stayed are accepting of the daily commitment that it takes to stay one within yourself, or they just need someone that is consistent in their lives.

Think about the issues that you had with your parents growing up, or the issues that you have with your own children as they grow up. As you reflect, think of the root issue: is one or both parties struggling with what is perceived as truth, or is one or both parties struggling with their identity? One of these will be at the root of the barriers within the relationship. Two people that cannot agree on what they should believe to be true is a barrier that frequently disrupts relationships. If you understand that truth in form must be defended by the one holding the belief, and that a peaceful disagreement may be the best solution, you are empowered to apply this knowledge as you either remove the barrier or bring light to the fact that a barrier exist. More importantly, you know why it exists. Facilitate the conversation so that it revolves around Source. This keeps you from attacking the other person. Instead, you are trying to view the source of their truth with them. If the Source is formless, you should be able to agree, and if the Source is man-made, respecting one another's views and the factors that lead to their thought process directs you to the appropriate approach to dealing with this barrier. If you cannot agree on Source that is not man-made, you must distinguish the difference between science being able to explain something versus being able to create it. The explanation of the Big Bang theory is much different than scientists creating another universe based on the scientific findings from that theory. Scientists have discovered exactly how and why it rains. They have broken down the process of precipitation and can predict from the sky when the rain will come, but they cannot make it rain themselves. This is the undeniable understanding of Source; that is the Formless Intelligence. Your relationship compatibility is largely based on who you see truth similar to. This is what makes the parent/child, sibling, teacher/student, and husband/wife relationships the most difficult. We all hold different truths in form; this will always cause division. However, can you see truth through the source of the Formless Intelligence where oneness can occur?

If the issue is at the root of an identity barrier, both parties must acknowledge that no one is perfect, but it is the commitment to becoming the ultimate self that separates one from another. Not operating as one causes a lack of cohesiveness within ourselves that obstructs our view of ourselves and others. Soul, mind, and body must be at the focal point of self-development. If a person is a hypocrite, a strong barrier will exist within their relationships. We do not have to be perfect in this development, but others respect when self-discipline is shown as we are working to become our ultimate self. People that identify with their body open the door to jealousy and insecurity, which turns into self-hate. This dimension closes off our ability to hear others because we are only focusing on one third of who we are: the body. This which means we are missing two thirds of the big picture. If a father pleads with his daughter not to wear a certain outfit, but the daughter does not listen, this is because she only identifies herself through her body. She knows that her body can be her identity if she chooses. Her body can gain her attention that makes her feel valued. Any relationship in this girl's life will revolve around her looks and body. This trains the mind to work against itself as it evaluates everyone else off of the standard of their body or looks. A significant other that is compatible with a person like this is likely to identify with their body and looks also. This would cause the relationship to be one dimensional and operating on a very low frequency.

Healthy relationships occur when the soul comes first because it is formless. It is the part of us that cannot be cloned. The presence of barriers in a relationship is due to the fact that both people in the relationship are not starting on a common ground. Think about your closest relationships and where the starting point is with you and the other person. Does it start in the soul and work its way to the other elements or does it start with the body and work its way to the other elements? The people that you are compatible with will mirror your starting point. If you identify with the body, you likely do what pleases your flesh, and other matters are secondary. Your close companions are subject to do the same. This realm may contain a lack of self-discipline, unhealthy eating, drinking, smoking, or it could be on the opposite end of the spectrum where plastic surgery and steroids are measures used to cope with a body you are not happy with.

Healthier relationships start with a healthier you. As mentioned above, become grounded in what is consistent which is the formlessness of who you are. Now we can offer an unchanging element to others, and a strong foundation is present for the relationship to stand on. Even if the other person or persons change, we can remain grounded, just as my mother did for everyone in her life. Our application of Truth and Identity can shine light on others as they will see the consistency in our life through the application of our knowledge on these matters. Understanding the relationship barrier allows our relationships to have a fighting chance against all that life will throw at us. Neglecting this truth leaves us with a predictable outlook on the future of our relationships with undesired barriers.

Wealth, Health, and Happiness Barriers (Purpose)

Wealth, Health, and Happiness were all placed together because they are all common things that we pursue. The truth is that these things can be defined differently for each person. But no matter what your definition of these components are, if we do not possess them in our life, it is due to a common barrier. That is the barrier of Purpose. This is where we can discover the age old question: What is My Purpose?

- Everyone has the exact same purpose. That purpose is to be in control of your mind, because thoughts in this realm become reality...a reality that is surrounded by unlimited resources to sustain itself. That unlimited resources are the thoughts that come from the mind. Both subconscious and conscious thought are activated and eventually become your reality.
- Say this: "My purpose is to be in complete control of my mind."
- Control of the mind teaches you to want the right things.

(Note the difference between your Purpose and your Fingerprint. Your purpose is to be in control of your mind. Your fingerprint is what makes you unique. This is our passions, strengths, interests, and our bodies. We all have the same purpose but each one of us has a different fingerprint, which is why the system is built to compliment itself. This is why we have doctors, waste management, teachers, zookeepers, farmers, pastors, bankers, and the list goes on.)

We are designed to be in control of our lives, and when we lose control, we are in an abnormal state because the level of control we have over our lives impacts how wealthy, healthy, and happy we are. If you work in an environment that you dread going to, and they control your time and finances, the lack of authority over your own life will cause you to have stress over what you do not control. In this case, it would be your time and your finances. At times, life presents an illusion that there is no other means to a desirable end for you. This strangles the ability to consider this thorough teaching. Understand this: If you are addicted to something, your addiction has control over you, and who you actually are is not allowed to make decisions in your life. This means that it is impossible for you to experience wealth, health, or happiness. Addiction only pleases the flesh, and you are now aware that this opposes the soul and the Formless Intelligence. We dedicate our entire lives to gain back control of what we have lost control of. Human life has become "The Pursuit of Control." But, what are you pursuing to take control of?

I do not know the area of your fingerprint. However, I can confidently tell you that if you are not in control of your mind, you are not fulfilling your life's purpose. Let us answer the question: In what area of life can my purpose be found? To be in control of our mind allows us to impact the world and community that we live in through our individual gifts. Imagine a person goes to college and gains debt, gets a house and car, and acquires more debt. The job they have will merely be used to pay back the debts from the education they received, the home they live in, and the car they drive. Nowhere in this system is there control over their lives or mind; instead they are controlled. This leads to frustration, anxiety, and misuse of time. Society has promoted that wealth, health, and happiness revolves around form. If you have adopted this Truth, we will not be able to agree on what constitutes wealth, health, and happiness. Being in control of our mind manifests itself by putting into form what is in our mind. Therefore, wealth, health, and happiness all come from our mind (not from the things have) because what is in the mind become the things that we have and the things we see. If we seek to gain control of your mind, then the things that you work for and worry about become things that are added to your life by way of a Mindshift.

You break the barrier of wealth, health, and happiness with **Purpose.** When you find your purpose, these three things will fit into your fingerprint. A person's fingerprint is what differentiates them from others. Growing up in a family of eleven children, we were hardly wealthy in terms of form. In fact, we lived in a four-bedroom house with one bathroom for the majority of my life. However, my mother would always say, " I am the wealthiest person in the world," with the biggest smile on her face, convincing us that she believed what she said. This statement would drive me to become angry because we had no money to acquire the things we, as kids, wanted. She would justify herself by saying that she had eleven healthy, beautiful children and the favor of God, which made her the richest woman on earth. We would eat dinner together as a family every Sunday and often invite friends or extended family over. I remember playing outside constantly with my siblings and neighbors, and when it came time to eat, everyone in the neighborhood looked to my mom for food because she is a great cook. She would feed anyone who came into our home, after they washed their hands! Every summer she would teach the kids of the neighborhood Bible stories and have us memorize scriptures and feed us all once more. She was in complete control of her mind and worked within her fingerprint, which is why she lived in abundance of wealth, health, and happiness. This was all accomplished with having very little in form or wealth that society tells us that we must have.

    My mother never had a car during my childhood. We would walk to the grocery store about three quarters of a mile from where we lived, carrying the bags of food in our hands or on our arms until we reached our home. We would walk and talk all the way there and back, creating some of the best memories of my childhood. One thing I remember most is coming home with the food, and everyone was given a partner and a job. In groups, we would help: peel the stem from the greens, peel potatoes, snap the ends off of the green beans, set the table, and the older kids could help cook. There was nothing better than Sunday dinner at my house growing up. I would imagine there was never loads of money in her bank account, but she was in complete control of her life and she was living out her purpose. I would venture to say that my mother would not have traded these moments for riches that the world offers. These experiences allowed her to achieve wealth, health, and happiness which she refers to as peace. I told this story to show you that this was accomplished without having a lot of money in the bank, owning a nice car, or having the newest widgets and gadgets. Amazingly, without all of those things, she had everything she had ever dreamed of because she achieved purpose within her fingerprint.

So how do you find your purpose when debt and having to work a job is almost a certainty in your life? It starts with redefining your view of the elements: wealth, health, and happiness. This must be done because it clouds your view of purpose. This is why every young boy wants to be a professional athlete, or every girl wants to be a model, movie star, or singer. What does wealth mean to you? Is your health a priority? What makes you happy or gives you peace? Once you can answer these in a formless way, you can move on to your true purpose. Wealth can be found in having control of your mind that has the ability to turn the invisible into things that can be seen. Wealth is being able to use your mind to overcome any environment or obstacle placed in your life without living inside of the torment experienced in that event. Health can be found in taking action on things that should be done for optimal physical function. Health is allowing your formless self to drive the motives for your physical action so that your stomach and mind are not what the body seeks to please. Happiness should then be placed as one's ability to be the master of their own time.

Finding your purpose is when what's on the inside of you connects with the outside world. For every person this is different. Sometimes it can be blatantly obvious in people while others must dig deep to find it. If what you are doing does not bring you joy, and you do not look forward to doing it everyday, it is not your purpose, and your fingerprint is not likely to be found in that job.

Having control of your mind is knowing that you have the mind power to change your reality. It is having faith that the Formless Intelligence is your source, which means whatever you think will manifest itself in form in your life—no matter what. What you think, your life will mirror. This is why it is important to have control of your mind, to control what you think, which plays itself out in real time throughout your entire life.

If you do not have control of your mind, your time is likely spent in these areas:

- Job
- Television
- Social media
- Video games
- Observing entertainment/celebrities
- Undisciplined eating/drinking
- Consuming unnatural stimulants
- Common social activities
- No physical or mental exercise
- No goals or visions
- Complaining

In each of these areas, a person does not think for themselves. It is important to recognize that everything is competing for the control of your mind. This is what makes the economy what it is. Being unaware of what is consumed allows society to influence what you will consume. This person will ride the wave of whatever is popular and acceptable. This type of person sees themselves as independent from their source. They do not regard the things competing for their mind so that the mind is subject to being controlled by many different form and formless elements. The company of this individual will mirror their own behavior, never allowing them to elevate above such simple matters. If a person does not carefully select what influences the mind, they will eventually accept what is only satisfying to themselves and neglect their moral responsibility. This person only consumes from the world, never putting their purpose back into the system.

If you have control over your mind, your time is likely spent in these areas:
- Reading
- Working within your purpose
- Building a business
- Writing
- Thinking
- Developing ideas
- Having growth conversations with others
- Exercising physically
- Disciplined eating/drinking

- Working towards goals and visions
- Traveling
- Solution-oriented thoughts
    - This person's entertainment revolves around their readings and thinking patterns. Entertainment outside of this is only given a limited amount of their time. Inside of one's purpose, they become producers, which minimizes time spent on what is consumed.

In each of these areas, a person monitors closely what they feed the mind. This person understands that the body ultimately becomes what it consumes through the eyes, ears, and mouth. From what is consumed, this person produces and puts back into the world things that will elevate others, even if their actions are the only things someone else sees. Controlling your mind increases your value, which will put you into the company of people that will continue to elevate your mind and body. The result of this is control over your life, which inspires you to produce more of what you were created for. Ultimately, this person understands the laws of the Formless Intelligence and applies them to their life, which allows them to have success acquired by predictable and repeatable systems. Due to the value created by the control of the mind, this person impacts the environment that they are in moreso than their environment impacts them. This means that they can be placed anywhere in the world and become successful due to the value created by fulfilling their purpose.

For the next year, use source and time intentionally. If you are not the fish in the sea, you cannot achieve wholeness, even if you are financially stable. Connect to the Formless Intelligence by respecting that something greater controls the universe, and you are connected to it! Outside of your job, fill your time with mind-growth activities mentioned in the list above. Find your fingerprint if you do not already know what it is. If you feel that you do not have a fingerprint or that you just can't find your niche, think of what frustrates you the most, and become the solution to that thing! There is a passion in every heart. What you "wish" you could do should be pursued in this mental space. Don't worry about your level of education, debt, or lack of finances. All that you need has been given to you freely: 24 hours, your Mind, Self-Discipline, and Vision.

As of now, barriers are no longer a blockage in your life unless you allow them to be. The barriers that are recognized for their valuable presence should remain unmoved.

- Your mind is full of thought…thought that is directed by the world, making your life a product of life's circumstances. Or your thoughts are governed by your own mind that is aligned with the Formless Intelligence

CHAPTER 2
SUMMARY

There is a powerful identity barrier that exists in the world that does not discriminate based upon age. Due to this barrier, we have allowed many things to steal our time. We must use our time properly so that the soul, mind, and body can become one. If there is a barrier between the soul, mind, and body, you cannot operate as one, which negatively impacts your ability to connect with yourself as well as others. Therefore, every relationship in this person's life suffers, starting with the relationship that they have with themselves, and filtering out to relationships with others. You must apply truth through Source along with your time in order to break this barrier.

This means that you are aware of and respect the Formless Intelligence as your sustaining source, which gives you a clear vision as to who you are. This vision will impact how your time is spent, along with what you allow to come into your body through your eyes, ears, and mouth. Things that enter the body are given to the mind and reproduced through thought.

A person should work to become one so that they do not have to change personas every time their sphere and environment changes. This instability confuses mind and body so that it will try to adapt to its environment. This is the opposite of what should happen. Identity through connection to Source empowers a person so that their environment is impacted by their identity and purpose.

There will be a barrier in every relationship if two people are not whole. People will always change and evolve, however, under the influence of your own identity, you get better at becoming who you are over time. This means that as an apple tree matures, it produces more of what it was created to produce; it does not suddenly begin to grow oranges. Likewise, as you age, you should become better at producing through the fingerprint of your purpose. Protecting the mind ensures that your fingerprint is not controlled by the world and used in a detrimental way towards yourself or your relationships.

Wealth, health, and happiness is pursued by all. Many times, in the pursuit, we must go from pursuing money and a stunning physique and set our minds towards our purpose and fingerprint, which will bring to us its equivalence in those things due to the increase of your value. If you live to chase wealth, health, and happiness, you will never catch it. However, if you find your identity and live in your purpose, they will come to you.

3

VICTIM

"Providing a solution to what you feel victimized by could be the solution that the world is waiting on."
-LaDrew Murrell-

Worth:

Before we venture into this chapter, I feel that it would be mutually beneficial to explore the worth of what is at stake. This will help information to be received with understanding, because of this foundation. Let's do a little practice to put a dollar amount on a few things you own! You are going to lose the following three body parts no matter what, however, you are compensated as much as you wish for what is being taken from you. What compensation would you like for the following?

Eyesight: $

Dominant Hand: $

Fifteen Percent of Your Mind's Current Capabilities: $

Total Revenue: $

Therefore, anything you are currently using your eyes to watch, your dominant hand to do, and what you give just a fraction of your mind over to, has a very valuable asset at hand.

(Although your entire body is far greater in value than the number we are using, use the total from the above exercise for this next practice.)

Now you have been welcomed to the Victimhood Resort. It sits beachfront on one of the world's nicest beaches and is all-inclusive with any drink or cuisine any person could request. Your stay is free as long as you remain the victim of your circumstance! In order to do this, you must relive the awful things that have occurred in your life that you have been victim to. The worse your story is, the nicer the room gets.

On this resort, there are many people, and all of their conversations revolve around what gained them a membership so that their victim mindset never leaves their minds. Every element of their body is used to embody what being a victim of circumstance or environment is all about. What each person sees, hears, thinks, eats, consumes, and does must connect to their experience as a victim.

Are you on this compound in your own life? Do you reside in the victim mindset? After all, the stay is free, and there is room for everyone.

In looking at this story, the asset is in owning the person. Your total dollar amount for only three body parts is far greater than the sum of a bill you could accumulate in a lifetime. In this chapter, think of that total dollar amount often and how worth it it is to protect the greatest asset you will ever own. Refuse to reside on the luxurious resort that victimhood offers. There is no feeling sorry for yourself here; we must progress. Let's begin.

Victim Mindset:

Being victim is a mentality that eliminates growth outcomes, but it is a very natural response to negative outcomes. Victimhood helps us accept our situation, given that we are the victim of circumstance having no choice to oppose the result. It provides a place of comfort in hardships through blame and lack of acceptance of consequences to our own choices. If we have been impacted by someone else's behavior, the victim mindset immediately finds its opportunity to settle into the mind. This aspect of our personality feeds on oppression, allowing us to live in this state because matters are out of our control. For example, one may blame God for their lacking or misfortune, allowing the state of victimhood a residence in the mind. This immediately eliminates the ability to understand the concept of a higher power due to a barrier in one's belief system. In fact, if we use the Bible for a historical context, the very first thing Adam and Eve did when presented with a conflict was blame, introducing the victim mindset as a response of self-defense to undesired consequences. Adam is asked why he ate what was forbidden, and he blames the Eve. Eve was asked why she ate the forbidden fruit, and she blames the serpent. Blaming takes the pressure off of you and places the fault elsewhere, making the victim mindset an easy place to rest your thoughts. There is no limit as to how long we can lay our troubles here. There is enough space in this formless room to hold every thought about every person you claim to be a victim to.

Delegating fault then becomes a natural reaction to negative stimuli, and our false identity is awaiting its next opportunity to act in this regard. This is the fish in an aquarium, or if you are lucky, you still live in the sea but have placed a bubble around yourself. This mentality lacks consciousness by providing a tolerance for residing in a mindset lacking solutions. If we accept this, we have become a victim of our own false identity, an identity that we have built for ourselves to protect us from the world. Here, we feel safe from the thoughts and opinions of others, which is always at the focal point of victimhood. This mindset enables a child victim of abuse to still be damaged as an adult because they held their experiences as part of their identity; the action became the makeup of who they were instead of an event that took place in their life. To remain in darkness allows your false identity to grow stronger, almost making it impossible to dis-identify with as you have made your mind believe that this is your true identity. More severe circumstances hold stronger bonds; those that are not self-inflicted become more difficult to overcome. By now, we know that our identity only comes through connection to the source, which is the Formless Intelligence.

As tragedy becomes more frequent in our society, everyone is subject to victimhood, empowering the victim mindset to become stronger than ever before. However, victimhood is not our identity. If we do not equip ourselves with the ability to recognize this mindset and correctly respond when it creeps into our subconscious mind, it will become our natural response to every unwanted outcome in our lives. These types of outcomes occur daily to large and small matters alike, but all encounters are either strengthening or weakening your connection to victimhood.

If you lost a loved one to the reckless behavior of another individual, this mindset will remind you each morning what your were victim to through that event. This becomes a daily reality that you live in. The hurt and pain that you feel ignites the mindset to hold on to the circumstance and you ultimately become it and embody all of the hurt and pain choosing not to let go. Being that tragedy is difficult to process, the innocence of those affected is the defense mechanism that the victim mindset uses to rule the subconscious mind and develop this persona. The recognition of this false identity does not make it any easier to overcome, but it gives you the tools needed to subdue it. It allows you to process what cannot be changed in a way that will not destroy your true identity or compromise your physical health.

If you identify as a victim and perceive yourself through this lens, you give yourself no control over your emotions, which interprets everything you take in. Because of this identity crisis, you cannot begin the healing process because your true identity has been lost due to outside circumstances. You must empower yourself with this finding: "Anything outside of you, is not you." This protects us from the things that happen to us that are unexpected and from the insecurities we all hold from our physical appearance. An unchangeable past and an unknown future will subconsciously keep you in the false realm of identifying yourself through an outside source that you are not. This gives a false identity power to rule in the darkness, which is the home of fear. In darkness, you may wish ill on someone who has wronged you as a coping mechanism. This only draws you deeper into the false identity and makes you and that person victim to the same situation. The more these thoughts are entertained, the more of a struggle breaking away from the victim mindset becomes. This counterproductive measure subconsciously takes you further away from the solution which lies within your true identity. Inside of the victim mindset, there are no solutions; you will stay in a place full of sorrow and blame.

It is impossible to be successful within a victim mindset. This is like being born into a false reality or being victim to a heartless act of another human. The unfortunate truth is that victimhood is strong enough to allow our residence in it to last our entire lifetime and the generations that come after us. In this realm, there is no control over a person's life. In this dynamic, you can only be one third of the three-part being that you are. This means a person's identity here will come from their environment or experiences. Taking on form as your identity takes away all power from your formless self. This is the fish that lives in or is born into the aquarium. This aquarium is equivalent to being born into poverty, extreme wealth, or having experienced an awful tragedy.

The goal of every human is to be successful. No person wakes up and desires to have a dreadful day, but waking up and choosing to have a victim mentality is choosing not to have success. Even if you are making choices in your subconscious mind, you are still held accountable for the choices that you make and the consequences those choices produce. All thoughts will produce the form that you see in your everyday life. Thinking in the subconscious mind is like this: A person doesn't feel they have control over their circumstances or over their life in general. They are overwhelmed and give up easily, denying the thought that their life can change for the better. No matter what they think or feel, their mind manifests its thoughts into form that becomes the life that person lives. Indeed, you do not have to believe in this phenomena in order for it to impact you. This is universal law that cannot be changed in anyway. Even if you are unaware that the victim mindset rules your mind, you are still subject to its effects. There is only one acceptable outcome to residing in the victim mindset, and that is to experience a lack of solutions, equaling lack of success.

The conscious mind works like this: A person is driving in an unfamiliar area and is pulled over for speeding. The driver tells the officer that they did not know the speed limit because they are not from the area. The officer replies that you are held accountable for upholding the law regardless of where you are from. Then issues the driver a ticket. Accepting this responsibility is not something this person is willing to do, so they knowingly and immediately defer by becoming the victim of the circumstance and place blame on anything they can think of to reason with the reality of the traffic violation.

To be a victim is to remain in the dark. Although you may not understand this at the time, this is by choice. It is like being born only to be dominated by the circumstances of life. Think of a young antelope that has never handled challenging situations well and could not even persevere as it was in the nursing stages with its mother. The antelope is later easy prey for a lion. It is as if it were born for that reason alone. This is how we are when we allow our personality to take on the role of victimhood as our identity. We are like the antelope that seems to have been born only to be dominated by life and become easy prey for the difficulties of life.

When a personality takes on the role of the victim for a person's identity, turbulence in their life can be linked to this aspect of their personality. If you recognize a weak moment within yourself, or notice others operating in the role of the victim, understand that the personality is feeding off of the opportunity of an unfortunate event to make its identity stronger than that person's true identity. Everyone must deny their personality the opportunity to connect with victimhood because it will try to connect with it any chance it gets. One may claim that they are overweight because it is hereditary, or that they ended up in prison due to the environment that they grew up in. Victimhood absolutely loves excuses, especially the good ones, and there are several great reasons that could validate someone's failure. Failure itself has no validation. We are all held accountable for our own success no matter the situation you inherit because the resources to overcome are available to all races, religions, or class of people. Work to become non-reactive to this false identity; this is how it loses power over you. Recognize it, but do not react with negative thinking. Accept its physical facts with the understanding that it does not define us and it is not who we are. Appreciate that physical facts can only change. Nothing of form can ever stay the same, so work to change the form around you to your benefit.

The biggest issue with the victimhood taking over your identity is that you can not produce anything. You are on earth to produce. Your fingerprint can produce something that no else can produce. As long as you are in victim mode, you will not produce anything. Chances are, you have already thought of the thing that you should have produced, but you have put no action to it. This is the thing that you feel cannot be accomplished due to lack of resources or the environment you live in. Providing a solution to what you feel victimized by could be the solution that the world is waiting on. The Formless Intelligence holds us accountable for producing in the system of life on earth; if we do not produce we prove ourselves to be invalid. We are charged to produce no matter what we inherit in life's circumstances. If we do not produce, we take away from the system without putting back into it. The impact this has on you can only be negative.

Think of a tree: as it lives, it gives us oxygen, shade, and fruit. When it dies, it gives firewood, homes, paper, and transportation. This creation gives and when it dies, it continues to impact the world even more, for generations. When the tree is connected to its source it will grow as large as it should and fulfill its exact purpose. As we know, some wood is nicer than others, but each tree serves us according to its "fingerprint". The tree takes from the earth, but from what is taken, much more is given, so it should be understood that giving more than you take makes you more abundant. We also could not progress if every tree's wood did the same thing for us. Like trees connected to source, we must all be different to make all things come together. We are charged to follow the same system while we live and when we leave this earth physically. When you leave earth, your presence should be felt in the same way as the tree, because what you left behind should provide others with information, wisdom, guidance, inspiration, and the like.

The victim mindset is a contaminant because it distorts the inside of you and creates a foggy lens for you to see through. This makes everything you see inaccurate. This lens contaminates how you see yourself and others, which means the reality that is created through the victim mindset can only be a false reality. This will ruin our relationship with ourselves and our relationship with others because eventually, we will blame the people that are closest to us. Although they had nothing to do with the event that led us into victimhood, we hold them accountable. The foundation for victimhood is blame. When our view is seen through a foggy lens, this is the fastest mechanism to cope with because blame is always within arm's reach of us. Let's face it, no one likes to blame themselves. So we blame others. If we are conscious and in control of our mind, we can quickly fix this thought by way of a mindshift.

Victimhood counts on the systems of the world letting us down. This mindset knows the vast differences from person to person, so that one man-made system cannot govern us all. In this way, victimhood relies upon the fact that we will not govern ourselves properly. The result is that we might blame the government or our environment that we are under for its poor systems. These same systems that we consider poor will be the same systems the victim mindset will have us wait on to fix the problem that drove us to the state of victimhood. The victim mindset disables the ability we have to govern ourselves appropriately, which is the only solution to defeat victimhood with.

The cleverness of victimhood is like this: We all know that one day we will die and become victims to death itself. So the victim mindset will create an identity around death. Although we ourselves are not death, victimhood will convince us that we are death which contaminates our character with the fear of dying. With death as your identity, through your foggy lens you see life incorrectly, and you may convince yourself to live it up while you can because you will die at a time that no one knows. Death as your identity creates your self-centeredness, and you party life away, abusing substances and indulging in as much sexual pleasure as possible. With this identity, you will take on financial gain anyway that is available to you. Consequences in this realm of carelessness could be: children are born out of wedlock, crime is unavoidable, drugs will be distributed, drugs will be abused, alcohol will be abused, we will mistreat ourselves, we will consequently mistreat others, and in the spectrum of death, we will do anything under the sun to look younger and live longer. There is no purpose in a person's life with a victim mindset because death will always latch onto victimhood, strangling your true identity, which is where your purpose lies. Therefore death will rule as the fundamental thought to every thought and action that follows. Here, death is in control of your mind.

Comfort Outside the Victim Mindset:

Evolving from the false identity of victimhood gives you the power back. You have gone from powerless to powerful in the matter of a mindshift. Understand that a mindshift can happen within a matter of a second! You may not think that anything feels better on this side or that anything significant has happened, however your thoughts in this realm operate in favor of what we want for ourselves. This allows you to manipulate the future from a state of control as opposed to being reactive to what the world gives you. All power from the victim mindset must submit to your new state: complete consciousness. This is where our subconscious and conscious mind work together as one. In this state, our conscious mind will be aware of the thoughts in the subconscious mind and send an alert whenever victimized thoughts are present.

Being in control automatically puts our situation at our will. Recognizing a harsh reality in the conscious mind puts our identity outside of the event that took place and allows us to see the situation as an event that has taken place, and not our personal identity. This consciousness gives us control, and we are designed to be in control of our lives. When control is lost, we work daily to regain authority over our own lives again. For example, if a person is in debt, lives in poverty, and has bad credit, they are not in control of their finances. Every financial related action they make is likely an attempt to gain control back in that part of their life. A person will work extremely hard for the money they earn only to pay it back to who they are in debt to, and they will do this until the debt no longer exists. Outside of the victim mindset, they know that they are not their debt. It is not their identity, and they are not the choices or other factors that led to their current state. Recognizing this give us the power to do something about it. Solutions can be examined to work towards canceling the debt. When the debt has been canceled, we regain control of our lives and are back in our natural state of being.

No matter how bad your situation is, do not accept the role of the victim. So, even if you are dealing with unwanted issues: debt, addiction, death of loved one, anxiety, depression, divorce, and the like, do not give in. If you do not see yourself as a victim, you are in control even in the midst of the worst situations. This is the case because the comfort outside of the victim mindset is control. This means it is possible to be in control even when it seems like we are not. By way of a mindshift, we are always in control of ourselves and our gifts. No matter how much debt, mental illness, or anything else undesired you have, nothing can take your true identity or the gift inside of you. So find comfort in knowing that your identity is protected by the Formless Intelligence no matter what happens to you, and you do not have to take on your situation alone or adopt it as your identity. There is comfort outside of the victim mindset.

Think of the toughest situation that you have experienced that has brought you into victimhood. Evaluate how you deal with the trauma it has brought into your life. Let's explore the difference between wearing the burden of victimhood and being free from it. Assume you are the fish in the sea that has created a bubble to swim into to protect yourself from the world. This is when you are in the state of victimhood, whether you realize it or not. As you attempt to protect yourself from the thoughts and opinions of others, you harbor hate towards whomever you blame for what has caused you harm. This negative energy literally eats you alive on the inside and creates false expectations for your support systems to meet. In this bubble, you are overwhelmed because your problems are too heavy for you to carry alone, but the bubble that you have created keeps them trapped on the inside with you. No one else can fit inside of your bubble, making it impossible for them to meet the expectations you have for them. In victimhood, if someone does not come to your rescue, there is no way for you to overcome. This compromises all of your relationships as your close friends and loved ones can never do enough to save you from the misery that you are holding onto as your identity. The comfort comes when you swim outside of the bubble and take a look at your troubles from the outside instead of from within. You will soon recognize that you are not alone, and you will see many others (including your close friends and loved ones) out in the open sea looking and reflecting on their own bubble that holds all of their troubles. You soon replace the comfort felt inside of the bubble with another form of comfort: control. You find solace in the many people around you that are affected by unfortunate circumstances. You will choose to serve them by telling your story or building a partnership for talking through life's struggles. This gives your conflict a purpose that can better someone else's life in a way that will bring joy to your own life. This joy you feel through the service of helping others is what provides comfort outside of your bubble.

When you find this comfort outside of the victim mindset, you see that everyone has a bubble that they created by the turbulence in their own life. However, the difference is whether or not they have made the bubble their home. This difference is what dictates the identity. Have you removed yourself from the bubble, allowing it to serve as a memory and testimony of what has been overcome? Notice that on the inside of the bubble you are alone, but in finding comfort outside of the victim mindset, you are not alone.

Consciousness Through Victimhood

Many times, it takes the difficulties in our lives to bring about consciousness. Consciousness comes when the voice or thoughts of the subconscious mind are recognized by the conscious mind. The conscious mind usually only acknowledges what your senses tell you. You have the authority to use this as course correction, not feeding the emotions and personality associated with the victim mindset. This means the problems that are faced in your life should be reflected on. Use them to show you where you are lacking effectiveness, which in turn gives you meaningful information that could lead to the solution. The unaware thinker is easily persuaded because they simply want to identify with something. Complete consciousness allows you to deny undesired responses that come initially. Instead, we can adhere to thoughts that lead to beneficial solutions. Light can be found here as we are learning to become aware of the subconscious mind. This shift in perspective allows you to see things through a different lens. With the proper mindset, you can now recognize that turbulence can be used to bring about consciousness in a way that may not have occurred otherwise. Now you have a respect and appreciation for the conflict that comes. It could be stated here that you have become better because of the difficulties that you have faced. These hardships brought a new way of understanding, and with a new way of understanding, a new way of thinking: thinking through mindshifts. Understand that this is not stating that you are happy that hardships come. Instead, you understand that it can provoke a powerful movement within you that used to be in a dormant state. This means our troubles in life are here to serve us, which indicates that they are beneath you. Our troubles are working for us only to bring us to a state of complete consciousness. If we see adversity in this light, it helps us deal with the unwanted issues each day. We must work to allow undesired events in our life to ignite the greatness within us.

The reality is that everyone goes through hardships. So the wise choice is to allow these things to work for you so that they serve a purpose that helps you become better. Understand that light brought into your life, no matter how it comes, is better than living in darkness. In the darkness, these same issues are allowed to serve as a stumbling block in your life. A person could complain about a certain situation or hold a grudge for an entire lifetime. If you pass away like this, you are sure to leave a stumbling block behind for the future generations to deal with, starting with your children, close friends, family, and onward. It is certain that problems will come. How you deal with them is your choice, and there are only two options: In the light that brings consciousness, or in the dark that brings victim mindset. Remember the most natural response is victimhood. You must act intentionally to reverse this way of thinking. This intentional action is called a mindshift.

The Formless Intelligence works within our universe perfectly as it continually provokes the consciousness within us. This means life will give us what it needs to stimulate our complete conscious state. If you ask why unfortunate things happen to those who are in the state of "complete consciousness," it is because no one is immune to the adversities of life. Everyone will experience difficult times. The difference is how you deal with what happens to you. If what was used in your life to provoke consciousness within you also provokes something great that comes out of you, the Formless Intelligence will seem like it is starting to work with you and not against you. If you do not chose to allow your adversities to bring light into your life, more adversity will show up because you have not evolved. If you are in the realm of darkness, you will continue to see adversity come into your life, and you will think that you can only accept it. Entering the light allows you to have an impact on whatever enters your life, and not the other way around. This is evolved consciousness.

Think about your life and the unwanted issues you have been affected by. Did you deal with them in light or darkness? If you are reading this, it is a sign that you are choosing to live in the light in order to live life effectively. Now that you are moving past the victim mindset, think of how your adversity amplified itself only due to your mindset when you thought as a victim. Victim thinking makes problems a revolving door, and they will seem to never go away as long as you think like a victim. You may ask, "Why does a parent lose a child to a tragic event, or why does a young child grow ill and pass away?" This content is not intended to cover why these things happen, but to recognize that bad things will happen in everyone's life at some point. Being prepared to handle these situations is in our best interest.

It is important to note:

- Being the victim separates you from consciousness.
- The Victim mindset is a **natural** response to defend your actions or take the responsibility off of you when unwanted consequences are at hand.
- **No solution** will be found in the midst of the Victim mindset.
- Things that happen in your life that cause turbulence should be used to initiate positive change in your life.
- Dealing with issues outside of the Victim mindset is in **your** best interest so that you will not lengthen the trauma from negative events.
- You will go through unfortunate situations in life no matter what.
- Victimhood is counting on you to mismanage yourself.

In the complete conscious realm, you understand that is unreasonable to only accept the good in life and not the bad. Whose life is only good? With no trouble, the good we have would not teach us to persevere, and anyone living must learn to persevere. No tough situation is enjoyed at the time you are enduring it. When time has allowed you to move past it, what you gained from it gives you more tools to face life with. These tools make you more effective at life. As you pursue what your heart desires, use what was learned from the hardships that you have overcome. Consciousness is rewarded by the Formless Intelligence. As you are becoming connected with the powers that align the universe, you will find life working for you in ways that are not by your doing.

It is recorded that Harriet Tubman brought three hundred slaves to freedom through the Underground Railroad. Since the number of slaves in America far succeeded that number, we are allowed to think of the difference between the mindsets between those three hundred slaves that chose to pursue freedom with her versus the mindset of those who chose to stay on the plantation. To give the due respect to those affected, I will only inquire of the three hundred slaves that left for freedom as it is safe to say that they did not see their identity in the state of victimhood. They opposed being victim so much that they risked their lives and their families lives in order to gain authority over their own lives. You could challenge the story of the antelope and say that these people were born to govern themselves and not be a victim of the circumstances of life that they were forced or born into. Stories such as these, as there are many, should serve as examples to us in our troubling times. It was also noted that Harriet Tubman never lost a runaway slave on her journey.

To use your worst point of conflict as a moment of awakening is a critical shift in conscious thought. Though it does not bring back the dead, you have made a positive thing come from a very unfortunate situation. Living in sickness or losing a loved one will never be desired, but what brings forth consciousness must be respected because it is consciousness itself that saves lives. So if a loved one lost their life, but it saved yours, be thankful. How much worse would it be for a loved one to lose their life and your life was not saved from it? Instead, you remained in the dark, drinking and smoking to cope with the loss. If a person lost a limb or their sight, but it strengthens their other limbs or senses, they have received an increase in their life. But, if a person loses their sight and their other senses do not develop stronger to compensate, the loss of sight did not serve a positive purpose. It is better to use adversity for the positive rather than not use it for anything good at all. All stages of the butterfly are necessary as each could be considered a shift in consciousness, and the end result is beautiful if you have the perseverance to endure until the end.

Consciousness comes from removing yourself from the bubble created by all of life's hardships so that you can reflect on what has happened to you or those that you love without carrying the difficulties of each circumstance on the inside of your bubble. Consciousness allows what comes into your life the time to strengthen you and reflect on the change. What is learned acts as a tool to take on the next task or to help build up someone else.

CHAPTER 3
SUMMARY

We have all been subject to the victim mindset, due to the severity of the circumstances that led us to it. For me, it was divorce and the losing custody of my sons. In this mindset, you only identify with things that are outside of yourself.

We should not accept our unfortunate circumstances as aspects of our identity. Instead, we should respect them as undesired events that have taken place in our lives. We should allow the darkness that enters our lives to provoke the light from within us to shine. If the darkness multiplies itself, we may never lose the grasp of victimhood. Then, we cannot recognize the light when it attempts to enter our lives in order to save us from the grasp of victimhood.

What happens to you is not always your choice. It may not sound empathetic to say that remaining the victim of anything is always a choice, even in the worse case scenario. Let's defeat the victim mindset and remove its power with our understanding and application of knowledge. We can use our entire body to take what once made us victims and use it to initiate the light that shines within us and impacts others.

Your body is the most valuable asset that you will ever own. You have ownership of your body, and anything that you allow to take ownership of your body and mind needs your permission to do so. The things that you are using your mind and body to do are controlling an asset that is invaluable. For you to control this asset consciously makes you invaluable. Understand your worth so that you do not allow yourself to stay in the state of victimhood.

4

OVERCOME

"Connection to the Source gives us unlimited resources to produce what our fingerprint is designed to produce; the universe will never run out of what you need. Therefore, we are left without excuse."

-LaDrew Murrell-

Leaving Victimhood Behind

In order to move past the state of victimhood, we must not allow barriers to form between us and the things in life that are desired. At this point, we understand the effectiveness of barriers and how they do not allow two things to become one. Victimhood keeps us from our destiny, so we must let it go. Our worst moments have provoked consciousness, which is the best thing we could choose to allow adversity to do. If we hold onto grudges that placed that adversity in our life, we are strengthening its barrier.

To move past victimhood completely, we cannot hold grievances against someone or something that we feel has impacted us in a negative way. Pity, blame, and hatred are all grievances that will take us out of the conscious realm and move the subconscious thoughts towards negativity and selfishness. Remember these thoughts create what you see in form. To snap out of it is to recognize the thoughts of the subconscious mind when they embody victimhood. Do not remain in those thoughts. Use a powerful mindshift into positive thinking. Imagine the fish that created a bubble around itself in the ocean. The fish sometimes chooses to go into its bubble and sometimes chooses to come out. The ocean is like the complete conscious thinker with unlimited resources, and the bubble in the ocean is the barrier that separates you from your true destiny. It is the choice of the fish where it should reside. The power first comes from the fish knowing that he can swim out of the bubble. You have done that, because you are reading this book! The challenge then becomes not entering the bubble again, and this is a daily choice that we all must make. If you find yourself blaming someone because of what you are enduring, or even wishing ill will on them, know that you are choosing to go back into the bubble. In the bubble, you are not free—you are a victim.

If you have taken on death's identity through victimhood, steer clear of its selfish and destructive thought patterns and behaviors. If you live only to please yourself because, one day you will die. This foggy lens will ruin your character. Your character is what is supposed to keep you from compromising and going wherever the wind blows. If we are not grounded, we are likely to live according to what the world deems as acceptable. This causes us to continually change our persona, and culture's trends change many times in the course of one person's lifetime. This is the most dangerous way a person could choose to live life. Understand that we will all pass someday, but death is certainly not who we are. We must govern ourselves accordingly.

Refer back to the list that was made in chapter two, and look at the things you blame for bringing you to the position you are in today. It is time to leave these reasons behind. These are the reasons why you are not. Now you have the information to turn them into reasons of why you are!

Victimhood to Wisdom

Suffering is the electricity to light. When you suffer from adversity, great or small, you must allow it to provoke new thoughts towards productive solutions. To do the opposite is to be lead by the flesh, which is one dimensional. The flesh is only reactive to what it comes up against; we cannot trust our instincts when we are lead by the flesh. Reactions in this state are costly in their consequences. Have you ever been in a fight or said something harmful to someone else? These are reactions from the flesh. These actions are reactive and negative. The energy and consequences that comes afterward invests itself in the trouble to come. Wisdom is noting that fleshly reactions are the most simple and common reactions. Although this is obvious, it is difficult to act outside of these common reactions.

A person only becomes wise by overcoming misfortune. A wise person is merely a product of the things they have overcome. So what is more valuable: the wise man, or the experience that has given him his wisdom? When you are in a state of wisdom, even your hardships are seen in a light that cannot threaten you. This is because hardships serve the wise; they serve and give the wise the information needed to overcome the hardship and win the battle. To the victim, problems compliment themselves by creating easy victories, inspiring more problems to come in and become victorious.

Wisdom comes from the soul because it is the opposite of everything that is easy, and your flesh wants to take the easy road every time. Wisdom and self-discipline are twins because a wise person must apply their knowledge to life consistently. To know and do are two different things. Wisdom opposes the wants of the flesh, putting the two in conflict every choice of every day. I am not saying that if you are wise you will not see misfortune, but when you are wise, you will find a purpose in the misfortune that comes to your life. Even our greatest point of conflict has a purpose. We can be assured in this because we cannot stop the adversity from coming no more than you can cure a terminal disease. Wisdom allows you to respond through the light inside of you where conscious thought dictates your thinking. This is when it is safe to trust your instincts because they are not reactive to the circumstances of life. Each situation is evaluated, and a calculated response is used to leverage the situation

Everyone experiences turbulence in their lives, which means every person is either a victim of their hardships, or they have become wise because of their hardships. Think about the adversity you have faced and whether you have become a victim of it, or if you have become wise because of it. Remember, being wise doesn't mean that that you agree with the adversity. Wisdom doesn't make it easier to accept adversity–it hurts all the same. The difference is that it only allows you to use it in a way that provokes positive outcomes to an undesired event. Wisdom does not mean less problems; it changes that way you respond to conflict in your life. When you apply knowledge, you will notice less conflict in the areas that knowledge was applied. As you have elevated your own thought process, the truth is that everyone is at a different stage in life. Due to this, conflict will always present itself. The people within your sphere of influence have barriers between them barriers due to the application of their knowledge compared to yours.

Wisdom through suffering is like this: A young man struggled with his sexuality, and he labeled himself homosexual. This way of life opposed everything that his family believed in. He was also raised in a way that caused him to believe that he was unworthy of life and love. He went through his entire youth and early adulthood lying to himself and those around him, and he contemplated suicide frequently. He finally decided that he would rather die than live life this way. At this extreme low, he challenged what was right and true. He came out to his family instead of taking his life. He found out that he was loved all the more. His family felt ashamed and sorrowful that he had lived alone with this burden for so many years to the point of almost taking his own life. His suffering caused him to apply this knowledge: love is more powerful than religion. Because of his wisdom, he is still alive today, and the victim mentality that he held for over twenty years was gone within a matter of a mindshift.

Someone might ask, "What is to be said about the individual that had a similar experience, but the reveal was not received with love?" The victory is in the freedom from the bondage of holding something inside that eats you alive. Being set free is the gift, and no one knows what it feels like to be set free if they were never in bondage. Wisdom surpasses false identities because your identity is formless. How that formlessness is expressed is the makeup of who you are. Therefore: one character trait, sexual preference, poor choice, great accomplishment, trophy, or successful career cannot define who you are. Wisdom through victimhood allows your identity to remain in its most pure form, which is formless. What the formless identity creates through its special fingerprint are simply expressions from the formlessness inside of you. You can not be defined by one aspect of who you are or one thing that you have done.

Beating the Victim in Me

Let me remind you that taking on this role is very natural, however, not producing is unnatural. You must ask yourself, "What have I produced?" Have you put into the world more than you have taken from life? Have you put into others more than you have taken from others? You beat the victim inside of you by producing, turning your thoughts into form. What you produce will be unique to your fingerprint and will be exactly what the world needs. Take action and trust your talents. As you rise in your mind, what you should produce will become more evident. Your purpose of being in control of your mind is equal to saying that every tree's purpose is to give shade and oxygen. What a tree's wood is to be used for is to be compared to what you are here to produce. Many different things come from the tree's wood. Through the manifestation of our fingerprint, we are held to this same principal. Or again, every tree has roots, and a trunk. This is comparable to your purpose. However, once the branches grow, the fingerprint of the tree is shown its leaves, flowers, or fruit that it produces. We must fulfill our purpose in order to produce the fruit that we are designed to produce. This all starts with connection to the source which is the Formless Intelligence. Connection to our Source gives us unlimited resources to produce what our fingerprint is designed to produce; the universe will never run out of what you need. Therefore, we are left without excuse.

If you are still unsure of what to produce, the answer is to invest in your mind by reading, thinking, and meditating. Produce mind power until your vision becomes clear to you. This is the invisible stuff that is powerful enough to create its equivalent in form. By producing mind power, we consume what other producers have made, contributing to the cycle until we ourselves become a producer. For example, this book (and any book that you have read) was produced by mind power from the author. Purchasing their work allows them to continue to produce by way of mind power. Mind power is essential to engaging in the cycle and your own self development. Even if it starts with you, the consumer of mind powered products. This will help prevent failing ideas. The Formless Intelligence only places its energy behind what your fingerprint is. Any work produced outside of your fingerprint will count on your long hours and hard work to keep itself steady. Working within your fingerprint makes you the commodity because your gift is what people are seeking. You could get this part wrong, so invest in your mind until you are sure of what you should produce. This will save you time and finances. This is much different than following the law of hard work. You can work tirelessly at anything and become efficient at it. You can always experience success due to dedication and work ethic. This does not mean it is your true purpose, because this person works harder than what is necessary. As a result, everything else in their life is in jeopardy of being poorly managed. Should a father constantly work and travel to make $250,000 per year, only to jeopardize the relationship with his wife and children? No, he should not. Isn't his family more valuable than a dollar amount?!

We should live our lives so that when we leave the earth, what we have produced can be as valuable as what the tree leaves us when it dies. Every tree leaves behind firewood. And all we leave behind a memory to someone. This is not enough. Life is much more than a memory. We need so many other things: tables, chairs, homes, boats, artillery, protection, government leaders, pastors, teachers, and global structure. From you, we need more than a memory. We need: inspiration, wisdom, books, modern solutions, cures to illness, architecture, leadership, and much more. If you do not have the resources to produce what you believe to be your niche, you must use the non-measurables that have been freely distributed amongst us as your bridge. Your time will become your most valuable asset, and what you spend your time on will allow you to beat the victim inside of you. Beating the victim inside of you does not guarantee riches in a material manner. There is no time in history that everyone became abundant in form all at the same time. This won't t be the case anytime soon either. What you produce in your fingerprint could simply provide you marginal income but inspire the very person that changes the world. In this way, you have not only left behind firewood, but you have planted seeds that will allow trees to grow until the end of the age. Everyone has inspired someone else to do something. Work to be the person who inspires the greatness inside someone else.

Predictability

Now we can see the victim mindset for what it truly is. Seeing victimization in a new light will not only change your perspective on hardships, it will allow you to understand that turbulence in life will come continuously. This fact is as much of a guarantee as death on earth. This means that we can predict that, at some point in our lives, we will be presented with an obstacle to overcome. After that one another will follow. It would be acceptable to ask, "In what area of my life will hardships come? Will I lose someone I love? When can I expect something that will come and shake up my world as I know it?" These things cannot be known. What is known is something will come sooner or later. This makes taking on the victim mindset a result of neglecting a natural law: the law that everything living must go through conflict in order to mature. This is actually a necessary part of growth and development because it improves the strength of the foundation on which the subject relies upon. Conflict in our lives grows us in the same way that rain and the rays from the sun grows our vegetation. In a sense, it is the very thing that gives us life.

If we can predict that hardships will come, it would be in our best interest to build a foundation within ourselves that will outlast any adversity that forces its way into our lives. Without knowing the: How, When, Where, Who, or Whys. This is how you build a foundation to withstand the unknowns:

- Perseverance
- Conviction
- Character

To outlast storms in your life, you must be abundant in the non-measurables of life. Since these attributes are formless, they can be acquired vastly. These are what will allow you to stand after the blows of life are taken at your core. These are areas that we can work on strategically. Focus to develop, as you are aware that you will need them at some point due to the laws of living. Perseverance is what allows us to endure the storm for however long it lasts. Perseverance is also needed to rebuild what was damaged by the storm after it passes. Laziness and compliance embraces the victim mindset so that perseverance becomes an unattainable abstract to someone. I assure you, anything that cannot be measured is attainable to all. It is within a matter of a mindshift. Your environment, mental condition, or addiction is not strong enough to keep perseverance out of your grasp. Attaining what is freely given is like this: A person believed they do not have enough time in the day to implement self-betterment strategies. The next day, they changed their mind and used the twenty four hours they were freely given in a much more effective way. So, if we looked at perseverance proactively, we could predict that it leads to success, which is also true. This makes success and failure as predictable as experiencing conflict. What is not predictable is how a person will react to conflict. Someone in the world has successfully overcome an issue that you are currently dealing with. So the question is: What is the difference between that person and you?

Different problems will come your way, and you may not be affluent in the areas that you are attacked at in life. In order to avoid becoming a chameleon for the sake of handling conflict, you must be convicted in what you believe, to the point that you would die for it. Conviction is like a parent willing to lose their life for the sake of saving their child's life in return. Conviction establishes and maintains a person's character no matter what situation may come. In this way, you do not have to change as life's circumstances change around you. Instead, you govern yourself based off of your convictions. Your character grounds you so that you will not move or be compromised by life or the temptations unjust gains.

To be empathetic to those who may have lost a loved one due to someone else's conviction to a religion, I will say this. Being convicted religiously is to be conformed to man-made ways that cannot be just, or justified. Religion is form because it is man-made. It is not wise to become convicted to a thing that you choose only because you agree with the source that it comes from. Proper conviction is much more difficult than this. It takes sacrifice because you likely will not agree with the Formless Intelligence, as this source only allows you to impact and react out of love and servanthood. No one prefers this way. Our flesh is too selfish and its nature is contrary to this suggested method. Have you ever driven past someone changing their tire on the side of the highway? I certainly have, many times. If you are convicted service and love would cause you to pull over and help them change their tire every time. It would also provoke you to give them enough money to purchase a new tire. Helping every single time you see a person in need would be your cause. This response embodies love and servanthood. To accept this way would not be easy. This is true conviction. Love or service cannot harm another individual.

When your character is firm in your convictions, you become non-reactive to the waves of life. Within a day, there are ups and downs that will take you on a roller coaster of emotions if you are not grounded. This is not saying that you do not feel happy or sad emotions. The predictability of life teaches us not to depend on the emotion felt during a specific time to be a stable place for us to dwell. Instead, we should appreciate the moment for whatever it brings into our life. No matter what happens, we can remain grounded because our character is found within our formless conviction. A person with strong character would not take a bribe or cheat to advance in status or wealth because predictability lets us know that a solid foundation cannot be built upon bribes or trespasses. When the storm comes, character founded on poor principals will leave this person destroyed by conflict instead of becoming strengthened by it.

When your character is firm due to your conviction, you cannot take on the role of a victim. You become like a person preparing for winter. Victimhood is not a part of the character of a person who understands and applies these values. Using what is predictable to guide you daily is simply a choice that takes a mindshift, at the cost of self investment.

Predictability works like this: A car manufacturer builds a car and counts on multiple failures to act as identifiers of areas in need of improvement. The knowledge of these failures are the indicators that eventually make the vehicle suitable to be driven by the public. So they test the car on multiple terrains, heat, snow, ice, and the like. After research is complete and the product is final, they put it to an even greater conflict; they crash the car into a wall. The manufacturer knows that you can only trust something that has been tested by many conflicts, and each conflict provides information needed to get closer to the final product. After thousands of tests and failures, they are confident that the car will not only get you from place to place but when presented with environmental factors or worse, a crash, it will keep you and your loved ones safe. The manufacturer becomes convicted in this belief and places their name on the car, because it has been tested through conflicts of all kinds. And the predictability of failure ran its course. Failure allowed the manufacturer grow in knowledge and craft. You later buy the car, a product crafted through many failures and conflict.

You are exactly like this vehicle, except you are the manufacturer of your own life. Now you can use the predictability of failure and conflict to work for you in a way that identifies areas suitable for growth, building you up to become the ultimate version of yourself.

Society often fails to use the predictability of conflict in the area of marriage, which can be supported by increasing divorce rates. Divorce these days has almost become as much as a guarantee as death. You, a family member, or a close friend will be impacted by this dreadful and life-staggering event. This is the case largely because we fail to use the predictability of conflict. Marriage is essentially a conflict contract. Marrying someone is stating that you will support that person through the conflict that they experience individually and that you also select them as the partner that you would like to endure conflict with in life. It vows that they are willing to stay with you although they will put you into conflicting situations ranging from small to large, and you will do the same to them. It is also stating that you will remain faithful to them as their bodies experiences conflict with time and gravity. You pledge to love them through all these things that we know are coming. However, we marry anticipating that only good times will roll in, and when the conflict comes, we run from it as if we are surprised that it showed up. I hope that you see the danger of not using what is predictable to guide your thinking. If you do not, it will ruin the purpose of conflict in your life. Just like the car, marriage will be put through many tests and eventually crash, but these things are what makes the bond stronger. After all, marriage is signing up for a partner to endure conflicting times with.

CHAPTER 4 SUMMARY

Victimhood is a false identity that seeks to own the lens that our view of ourselves comes from. However, the recognition of this false identity allows us to process what cannot be changed in a way that does not compromise our true identity. The false identity that victimhood provides forbids us from producing, which makes our lives ineffective. No one should take more from this life than what they give to the world through sharing their purpose with others.

Use a powerful mindshift to switch into positive thinking. This is all that it takes to leave victimhood behind. Although playing the victim is going to be the natural response to unwanted things that come into our lives, we are not victims. To be a victim is a choice, a choice that we will no longer accept as our truth or our identity.

Suffering is the electricity to light. When you suffer from adversity, great or small, you must allow it to provoke new thoughts towards productive solutions. To do the opposite is to be lead by the flesh, which is one-dimensional. The flesh is only reactive to what it comes up against; we cannot trust our instincts when we are lead by the flesh.

Instead, allow conflict to provoke consciousness within you. Light and consciousness brought into our lives, no matter how it comes, is better than remaining in the dark. What brings forth consciousness should always be respected because it is consciousness that allows our purpose to be found. Make note of these statements:

- To take on the roll of the victim is the most natural response that conflict will entice you with.
- Victimhood tries to link your identity to ONE of the many things you may experience in life: race, religion, death, environment, socioeconomic status, and the like.
- A person in the state of victimhood is not employing wisdom.
- Victimhood distorts the view of life. This causes you to see the world and yourself through a foggy lens.
- Govern yourself in a way that makes you a producer. It is impossible for a victim to produce.
- Use what is predictable to guide your next steps and prepare for a future that is only partially unknown. Build your foundation on perseverance, conviction, and character. Strength in these areas will help you avoid the snare of victimhood.

PART 2

5

GREATER VERSUS LESSER

"If we can understand this dynamic, we can more effectively govern ourselves and become one so that we might live a life that is desirable according to our own understanding."

-LaDrew Murrell-

The contrast between greater and lesser is one that I suggest we discover and bring into our conscious thought. Everything that we know, understand, and accept functions around this constant natural law. What is lesser is dependent on what is greater, and it needs what is greater in order to increase itself. Nothing or no one serves what is not greater than itself. This hierarchy is the motive behind evolution in all realms of what lives. This dynamic is found in all things that are living, and also in what is governing life. At all times, something is greater than what is seen, and what is seen is always dependent on what is unseen. In other words, what you cannot see is greater than that which can be seen.

Let's first look at the two great lights: the sun that lights what is called day and the moon that lights what is called night. We can find truth in this concept as one light is greater than the other and the lesser light is dependent on the greater light to fulfill its purpose. The sun gives life and light to what we call day, and it is greater than the moon which only shines because it reflects the light from the sun. The sun's light shines on it and the moon, and the moon reflects its light to the earth. We call this night. This fact is evident in the relationship between the two lights as they very frequently acknowledge one another. They set and rise each day being visible at the same time, collaborating and accepting the role that they each fit into. This phenomenon distinguishes purpose and time, because the moon must acknowledge during this time what is greater than itself. It daily humbles itself in the presence of the sun, which is greater. However each light is given its appropriate time to shine on the earth so that there is a balance which creates desired harmony on earth.

If we gave human characteristics to these lights, it would be fair to state that the moon envies the sun and its brightness. This relationship balance puts them in conflict with one another due to the hierarchy of the relationship.

Nothing ever wants to take on the role of the lesser. This dynamic would cause the sun and moon to fight for the attention of planet earth which they both shine on in their appropriate time. During the spring equinox, the sun dominates the day shining on the earth for more than twelve hours daily, winning over the favor of the people because of the harvest it brings. But, during the winter equinox, the moon reigns as it dominates with night, minimizing the time the earth receives light from what is greater. When the moon reigns over the earth, you must gather and store up the harvest until spring returns, because the lesser is in control. This greater and lesser dynamic is a daily battle, but what is greater and lesser is each allowed its time, and an opportunity to concur each day. The presence of both lights cannot be hidden or denied, and one without the other would only result in an unbalance which would create something extremely undesired. Therefore, it is in the best interest of what is living (in form) that what is greater and lesser work together as one. To do the opposite creates a contrast that allows neither to operate at full capacity to enhance life on earth.

So then, what is greater should not dictate because it needs the lesser in order to function in a harmonious way. This is in the benefit of both the greater and lesser. Your form is lesser, and the formless part of who you are is greater, but they must work in a harmonious fashion together to provide you with healthy life experience just as the sun and moon must work in a balance that provides life on earth. Your formless self is not dependent on what is lesser; instead it is limited by your form, however, it needs your body to function on earth, creating a partnership that requires two working parts to become one. They must acknowledge each other daily and each function seeks to win the day. This is done by dominating the time that you spend in either the greater or lesser realm. What is lesser seeks to own the day just as the moon does but without regard to the greater function. The lesser self would destroy your form which allows you to live, only to please itself. So then, there is a dynamic within you that is worthy of your understanding and time. Each aspect seeks and deserves an opportunity to express itself, however, the only beneficial expression happens when they are unified. Otherwise, the flesh expresses itself freely because it is not in contact with the formless self or the Formless Intelligence. The formless self cannot express itself outside of the body without the permission from the body. This gives the upper hand to what is lesser all of the time. This means that you are figuratively always in the winter equinox until you find harmony within your greater and lesser self. To become one is the goal of greater versus lesser. However, the contrast must be seen in a conscious light because of the natural difference between the two elements. Therefore, becoming one is a daily challenge as one continues to compete against the other because what is desired by each can only contradict the other.

In moving forward you must recognize and understand that there is a soul inside of you that is invisible but very real. It has a voice that only you can hear, and a conscience that seeks to guide your actions. It knows everything about you and was present whenever you did the things that no one else knows about. But your flesh has the overriding authority to connect with the universe because it is made of form, just like the world. Your form seeks to connect with the form of the world, which is how we are all similar in the things we desire: winning the lottery, living in a big house, having a nice car, having the perfect body and height, beautiful looks, friends, status, more money, and all the wonderful things life has to offer in form. But the soul seeks to gain more of what is formless: love, time, compassion, perseverance, integrity, peace, selflessness, and the like. This creates an interesting contrast that we all deal with differently as we are all seeking to fulfill the multitude of desires that we have. But what desires are we working to fulfill, those of the flesh or of the soul?

If we can understand this dynamic, we can more effectively govern ourselves and become one so that we might live a life that is desirable according to our own understanding. The cost of this is consciousness through self-discipline and mindshifts. Now that you have obtained authority over complete conscious thought, what was once used to work against itself, prohibiting optimal function will now become one all within a matter of a mindshift.

The Lesser Part of You

What is lesser always connects with form, which can only last a moment in time. Your flesh is the abstract within life that I am referring to as the lesser part of a greater system. What is lesser in us is relatable to all mankind and also very predictable because the flesh has evolved to seek what is only pleasing to itself. The lesser lacks regard to the physical and sociological damage the behavior may cause. Your flesh is also reactive to its environment. This attribute constitutes predictable behavior. The acts that are self-pleasing contribute to what is already destined. It speeds up the process that brings death to what lives in form. Place no hope in what is lesser, but find comfort in the understanding that we are not alone in the things we struggle with. There are many other people (living and of the past) that have dealt with or are dealing with the same issues that you are currently up against. Anyone in a body battles with similar hardships to someone else; you will not be the first or the last to go through your adversities.

Not only is the lesser part of you predictable, it is allowed to govern a certain part of your life called youth and young adulthood; such as the moon dominates during the winter equinox. This is due to the barrier of age against knowledge and understanding. So the terrible twos will always be a problems parents face. Even past those days of our youth, the flesh seeks daily victories just as the moon has been given access to rule over the earth daily. So what comes natural to the flesh is: lack of identity, greed, envy, dishonesty, sexual misconduct, self-ambition, rage, substance abuse, and the like. This starts at infant stages, which is why a toddler identifies with their blanket and does not want to share their toys. It evolves into adulthood in a more destructive manner. But we know that the earth without the moon would equal disaster, so how do you function in a flesh suit, that would seek what is damaging over what is beneficial if it had its way?

You must not allow your moon, or the flesh, to be the dominant force of who you are. Ask yourself this question: Would you give up what is false for what is true? The answer you choose is very important, but being aware of this choice is the beginning of becoming one. Can you even name one thing that the flesh seeks that will last forever? You may say love; but what does the flesh love? Another person? That person will surely die one day. Or the expression of love. However, love in its formless state is a contradiction to the flesh. You now understand what is true through Source, so now we can define anything with a man-made source as a changing and preferred substance. Being addicted to something and not knowing you are addicted or not caring because the addiction satisfies the flesh is like siding with what is false over what is true. Being addicted, knowing there is a problem, and wanting to be released from that addiction is to choose the truth over what is false. Even if you are still addicted at the current moment, you have chosen what is true. This is the first step in the mindshift that brings life by neglecting the wants of the lesser.

The lesser part of you seeks to dominate your life until your form dies. If you allow it to control you, you will live a life that does not seem to progress. What the flesh seeks is not based on age; it wants more of what was listed above: money, power, jealousy, anger, sexual fantasies, intoxicants, drugs, and the like. So a person governed by the flesh may seem to be connected with who they were in their youth for an entire lifetime. They might not ever evolve past these simple matters. The lesser self stumbles when these things present themselves, because no matter who you are, these things tempt the flesh even if they are not acted upon. If you are reading this, your flesh connects to at least one of these areas, if not more, so you understand how this temptation works. The lesser self is completely reactive in response to life because it only uses the senses to connect with life. In this way, if someone cuts you off in traffic, and it makes you feel angry, you may immediately react by honking, showing an unfriendly gesture, or speeding up to cut them off. This shows how the lesser self is reactive to form outside of itself. You may remember a certain smell like that of an apple pie, and it may remind you of your grandma's house in the summer. Anytime you smell or see an apple pie, it takes you back to the place associated with what your senses connects with.

Understand this: Your form is predictable, and what it seeks most of the time is not beneficial to you, but often, what is sought after enhances death. That is guaranteed to all living things on earth. Your form has the power to limit you by controlling your actions based off of its desires. It is extremely close to the outside world, so it seeks to manipulate the world to acquire what it wants. A flesh-first mentality makes it nearly impossible to become one within your soul, body, and mind. Therefore, this type of person operates as one third of who they actually are, leaving the mind, and soul to work against the body. It is not in your best interest to submit to your lesser government, because selfishness is the opposite of what you should be convicted in. To become grounded in the flesh is to live a predictable life: reacting to things as they occur and constantly chasing after the things that make you feel good. This also produces predictable outcomes that inspire yourself and others to stumble along the path in life's journey and learn tough life lessons that sometimes end fatally…. or even worse, end fatally for someone affected by your behavior.

Your lesser self has no discernment for consequences to actions. Your form is not aware of the formless world because its senses does not allow the flesh to understand such things. Therefore, an activity as simple as smoking is seen through the foggy lens that says, "I enjoy this," "I am addicted to smoking," or "I prefer to fit in with the crowd." Whatever statement that is made to validate the act of smoking is made in a state of distorted vision. Nevertheless, the harm smoking does to the body means nothing to the smoker because the flesh seeks to win the day by engaging in activities that are pleasing in the moment. Eventually, these behaviors become habit, and addicting elements gain an easy gateway into the body, causing you to latch onto the endorphins you receive from the stimulant of choice.

To chose the path of the lesser is to knowingly choose self-destruction. Unfortunately, self-destruction to the lesser can be seen as a way out of the misery of life as you know it. This is done without recognizing the greater consequences to the behaviors that are selected by this aspect of who you are. This means of self-destruction is also seen as fun because these activities make us feel good physical and emotionally. Use the predictability of the lesser self in order to combat its desires. This means you will place a formless barrier by strategic planning between you and your lesser self.

The Greater Part of You

What is greater is formless. What is formless is not dependent on form just as the sun does not depend on the moon. However, it is in the best interest that the two functions operate as one here on earth. Since what is formless does not have form itself, it does not seek to connect or identify with the form of the world. Neither is the greater tempted to engage in activities that are pleasing to the flesh. What the greater part of who you are can do for you is immeasurable because it is formless. Your soul does not live to please what is temporary, but it desires to use what is temporary to produce good things that will contribute to more people living in a way that inspires others to live life governed by the Formless Intelligence. Your greater self is reflective of the information you take in so that you can not only monitor your thoughts but also make a calculated decision on what action should take place based on the formless impact of the action. Only what is formless can stand the test of time. This is why we forget people unless what they left behind was formless and in abundant measure so that form could not contain it. Names like: Jesus, Nelson Mandela, Muhammed, Gandhi, Mother Teresa, Adolf Hitler, and Siddhartha Gautama (Buddha) all left an abundance of formless abstract that could not be contained, which is why they are still followed to this day. This formless power is what the soul is connected to.

The contrast between what is greater and what is lesser literally opposes one another in every way imaginable, creating the dynamic of competition for the mind. What is greater seeks love, faith, hope, peace, gratitude, generosity, service, discipline, and wisdom. These abstracts are difficult because they do not please the flesh. Although they may be good for you, utilization of these features do not always feel good to the body or fulfill the physical needs of the flesh. To be able to use these measures takes self-discipline, practice, and patience, just like mastery of anything beneficial.

You must work to allow the formless part of who you are take over your life so that you may govern yourself in the realm of complete conscious thought. This means you embrace things that are not fun, and you use this as an indicator that you are doing the right things. No matter how much you lift, leg day is never fun, but it is extremely beneficial. And soon enough, you will look forward to the feeling of defeat from a great leg workout. Through this mindshift, thoughts that are displayed produce its equivalent in form and formless abstracts. The difference is that you are aware of the choices that are being made and use predictability to anticipate the form that follows formless function. Since your life is a product of the thoughts of your subconscious mind turned into form, it is in your best interest to be aware of and governed by the greater presence of yourself, which is also formless. It is guaranteed that you will face turbulence in your life, and it will happen more than once, making perseverance a key element to success. Knowing this, it is wise to take action by recognizing your greater self as one that can provide the ability to let these trying times serve you with knowledge and understanding of life. This will aid you in becoming your ultimate self. This can only be done in the formless realm of your greater self because it does not react to the negative stimuli that will come time and time again. Instead, it reflects and calculates the best way to navigate through form and formless barriers. So when you are presented with tough circumstances, or even great successes, let your greater self lead the way.

Your soul is what is connected to the Formless Intelligence, giving you access to a complete mind and a healthy body that can properly manage the desires of the flesh. This person when given money, power, and influence will properly manage those elements under their greater influence, provoking others to become better themselves. This is just like the sun shines so that everything that receives its light can grow, travel, and mature to become everything it was created to be. You may ask why the body even matters if the formless is so good. This is because on earth you need a body, or else you cannot relate to or manipulate the world of form. Your soul and the Formless Intelligence are in need of your body to work within the world of form. Think about love. When it is formless, it is perfect; but to take on form, it needs a person to express it. If love is expressed from the greater self, it is beneficial to others, while the same abstract expressed in the flesh could be the opposite.

Understand this: Your soul cannot have power without complete conscious thought. Being in control of your mind in this way urges you to remain in control because it takes only a unconscious mindshift to lose control and become led by your flesh. To remain in the light is very difficult because you must fight against the easy way, which is pleasing the flesh. This must be done in order to remain in the realm of the greater presence. You must be willing to deny what your body wants to do in order to embrace difficulty and walk the narrow path. To embrace what is displeasing to the body does not become habit. Only self-discipline with a large dose of perseverance can lead the way. If you were led by your greater self, you would have all of the things that you want in form without compromising your integrity or character for it.

Your greater self not only knows everything about you, it knows all of the things that you can no longer remember. Your greater self is also in connection with the unknown information within our universe. The stakes are much higher for this greater government as it is held responsible for the awakening moment in your life. It attempts to use each form of conflict as the factor that leads to consciousness. What is greater is held completely responsible for what the flesh does, whether you are conscious of your actions and their respective consequences or whether you live in a state of unawareness and do what is self-pleasing. The greater self, although it is formless, powerful, and has the ability to be complete by itself, cannot reach oneness without the flesh submitting to its will. This makes the flesh slave to its desires and not the other way around. And since the greater cannot make the flesh do anything, it uses conviction through character to carry out its mission. At all costs, your greater self will work to improve you; it thrives on the conflict that comes in daily because conflict is what keeps the lesser dependent on the greater. However, this conflict can be found in things that bring success or failure; conflict is the key ingredient to growth. Conflict is the water in the process of planting and the harvest.

Although, what is greater is not dependent on what is lesser in order to be greater; it is dependent on the lesser to live effectively in order to achieve oneness in a way that produces desirable outcomes for all within the sphere of influence of that individual. This oneness is what the

Formless Intelligence requires all of nature to adhere to at the consequence of self-detriment.

You have heard that you can accomplish anything you set your mind to. However, this is a partial statement. The greater part of you is like this: Formlessness does not need money because it can produce things that attracts resources, like money. Through this formless leadership anything in form can be attained. People work their entire lives to own things like a home, car, boat, business, or land, but fail to own their own mind and body. Driven by fleshly desires, they work their entire lives to own material things while their formless powers lay dormant. Whenever conflict is able to be used in your life as an awakening measure, the formless structure of yourself takes over and all of the things in your past become useful in pursuing your future in a state of consciousness. And what is greater uses the activities and experiences of the lesser part of a person's life to create a self-generating system that acquires more of what was desired all along.

Stronger

One of these dynamics is stronger than the other. In the contrast of greater versus lesser, the strength of one overpowers the other so that when a thought comes to the mind, action ensues from the stronger of the two elements. This means if your flesh is stronger than the greater part of you, then goals, dreams, and aspirations are going to seem to be impossible to accomplish because the means to get there is not possible to someone who is incapable of persevering. In this scenario, someone might know the best route to success, but action towards what is greater is ruled out by the lesser flesh.

If your flesh is stronger than your formless self, victimhood is the only reasonable option, as the flesh can only identify with things on the outside, things of form. This means situations, environment, other people, and anything else outside of yourself will make up the concluding factors of everything that you deal with. The Formless Intelligence is not controlled by the form of anything, which leaves all of your desires as a possibility.

The only reason that you are not doing what you dream of doing is because your lesser self is stronger than your greater self. This is the only difference! To change this will take a conscious mindshift as you decide to become greater than the fears (which are outside of your body) that have inspired you not to become everything that you know you could be. To help illustrate this point, and drive the action that takes place in your life after reading this chapter, I offer this story that shaped my life as I knew it.

As a young boy, I went to school with predominantly white kids and predominantly white teachers. I had tons of friends, and my elementary and secondary educational experience was conducive to furthering my education at the next level. Unfortunately, I did not see things this way because I did not experience or see people that looked like me holding positions of power or influence. With this mindset, I connected with what was lesser and defined my life based on experiences outside of myself. I literally believed that I was not capable of being "smart" due to the fact that I did not know anyone of color that I deemed as having a job that a "smart" person would have. Growing up, I did not see people that looked like me holding certain positions: teacher, dentist, pediatrician, coach, principal, banker, lawyer, and the like.

I ruled out these types of careers for myself because my understanding led me to believe that black people only became music artists or athletes. This idea was supported by the fact that I was always one of the better athletes in my class. Due to my speed and instincts in sports, my friends' parents would recruit me to play on their sports teams, and the coach would pay the registration cost for me to play for his team. This evolved into me not trying very hard in school, simply because I allowed everything outside of myself to dictate everything that I would become. As a first Team All-State football player, and a State winning track athlete in high school, I received no NCAA offers due to ineligibility. I scored a seventeen on my ACT and had a 2.0 GPA.

It is easy to see that my lesser self was much stronger than the greater part of who I am. I had the see-it-to-believe-it mentality, and since I did not see people that looked like myself holding high paying professional positions, I did not believe it was possible for me to do either. I allowed my environment to become my identity. This continued to shape the lens that I viewed life with.

What outside fear is keeping you too afraid to pursue your purpose? We all have a list. Let us take a moment to identify the outside elements that are out of your control that hold us back. In a perfect world:

Where would you live?

What would you do for a living?

How much money would you make in a year?

What would you look like physically (factors that are within your control)?

    These are a few very simple questions that have everything to do with greater versus lesser. Whatever aspect of yourself is greater dictates how these questions are answered. Use the answers to the questions above to identify if you are allowing circumstances that are not YOU to dictate your life. The only things stopping you from becoming who you desire to be and acquiring the things in life that you wish to have is a certain way of thinking based upon what can be seen. Let us take action and shift our minds towards what is greater.

    There is only one way possible for someone to live a life that is less desirable than they hope for: allowing your lesser self to become strong enough to take away all of the things that you wished that you could acquire or obtain. In the same, there is only one way possible for someone to live a life of authority without the threat of having everything stripped of them: allowing your greater self to become strong enough to develop your fingerprint, which increases your value. A person's fingerprint has to follow them everywhere that they go. Because of this, no matter what the economy looks like, or the vulnerability of their position at work, a person's matured fingerprint is stronger than any adversity that can be presented by their lesser self.

    I wish to share another story with you to serve as evidence of this finding. In my last year of education (which is the same year that this book was written) I began to teach and communicate with my students from a different lens. I could feel that my time in education was coming to an end due to the waywardness of the public education sector, so I began gathering information from what I observed and my conversations with students.

    The school that I taught in was 40 percent non-caucasian, however, there were only two teachers that were non-caucasian. This means that less than 3 percent of the staff looked like the student body. I met with human resources to address my concerns. In a thriving school district, this school was underperforming, and the achievement gap continued to widen. To accommodate this, the school was placed on a redesign term to "fix" the issues. This fix was an attempt to address what was seen: failing test scores, tardies, absences, behavioral issues, and low student engagement.

I knew that the problems that we were facing resulted from elements that were unseen. Failing test scores, tardies, absences, behavioral issues, and student engagement were only a result of poor connection between teachers and students. In turn, poverty created an environment that made the lesser much stronger in the lives of many of these students. This brings to mind a student that was struggling academically. He was also on a behavior contract, so he was closely monitored by each teacher every hour of the day. This student requested to work with me in the mornings to make plans for a successful day and in the afternoons to debrief on how the day went. As we met over the span of a few months, our connection grew strong and trust was built, which resulted in deep and real conversations. I did not have this student in class, but we spoke often in the hallways and cafeteria. I eventually asked him why he chose me to be his support teacher; he did not even have me as a teacher. His response was that he felt like we would get along. In other words, I was the only teacher in the building that looked like him.

I eventually learned that his father walked out of his life, which resulted in he and his mom moving year to year as their lease would end. His problematic behavior stemmed from an environmental factor and an empty void on the inside. After many discussions about his father, I supported his decision to reach out to his dad by phone. When we met in the morning the next day, his eyes began to water the minute he saw me. He said that his dad answered the phone but after the young man said "Hello," his father hung up on him. With tears in his eyes, he asked me if I had a dad. Seeing his pain, I almost broke out into tears myself. I asked him what made him ask me that question and he replied, "Most black men don't have dads." This understanding made his environment stronger than his greater self, which resulted in poor behavior and poor academic performance.

I will share another story of a young man who was under the influence of what is lesser so that he engaged in behavior that showed no regard for his life or the lives of others. I had never had this student in class, but his reputation was well known by everyone around the school. He eventually could not travel the hallways without an adult right by his side. Despite this, he had always showed me respect and I displayed the same. In the redesign plan, teachers were able to offer special classes where any student could sign up for specialized learning opportunities. This student signed up for my class on several accounts. This led to some of my most memorable conversations as an educator.

One day, I asked the young man why he was throwing his life away. He replied, "Because I don't care about my life." I asked him if he believed if anyone cared about him and he replied, "No one cares about me. Well, I guess my grandma does." I went on to tell him that I cared about him and believed that he had great potential, especially in sports. He was by far the most athletic middle school student that I have ever seen in my tenure as an educator. I asked him why he would throw such great talent away, and I told him that his family would love to see him succeed. I explained that life was rough for a lot of other people also, but in order to become successful, he would have to find a way to overcome whatever he was dealing with. I explained that jail cells do not care who occupies them as long as they are filled. I asked him about the gang that he was a part of from the trailer park, why he chose to be a part of that organization, and if he was aware of the future consequences of his actions. What he told me blew me away: "I know what I am doing, Coach. It doesn't matter what happens to me because I have nothing to live for. My mom has been on drugs since I've been alive, and my grandma is stuck with me. I bet she doesn't want to be stuck with me either. I've never met my dad, but the guys in my neighborhood are nice to me, so I do the things that they do. I literally have nothing to lose. I tried praying to God so that he would help me, but nothing happened. Do you believe in God, Coach?"

His environment and other outside elements became what he believed in, making them much stronger than what was on the inside of him. I knew in my heart that if he were in the proper environment, even now, that the kid would be just fine. Due to his age and his environment, I knew that a mindshift towards something greater was extremely rare statistically. So I ask you:

Are you similar to the people in your environment?

Do you influence your environment or does your environment influence you?

Have you defied the odds in your own life?

Based upon how your environment has impacted you: Under similar circumstances would you have been similar to the students in these stories?

The only suitable option is that we strive to become what is greater so that our environment, physical condition, or physical appearance does not become what we see in the light of truth. Nothing can defeat what is stronger than itself.

Free

I used to think that life was not fair. I grew up on free lunch and food stamps. Yes, I may have been signed up to play sports, however, I played in shoes that were too big because I was given what was passed down to me from my older brother Larry. I also did not have the internet or a computer at home to complete homework assignments when I was in high school. These are merely a few reasons that explain why success was not a likely end in my life.

Unfortunately, we are all without excuse because formless things come without a price tag. Therefore, we are without excuse as to why something cannot be done about our situation. When we allow our environment or circumstance to guide us into our lesser selves, things are not free under this identification of self. Things such as: needing a new car, money to pay bills, medical expenses, tuition, taxes, and the like all cost money and use up resources. Worrying about these things would cause anyone to become anxious about their future.

Formless things have placed a chasm between you and the impossible! What is needed for you to triumph to victory is free and available to all? It only takes a consistent mindshift over a period of time to change what was into what should be. Life charges you nothing to think differently, and this is the action that will change your life as you know it. At times, the solution to your issues are simple enough to miss for an entire lifetime, such as thinking differently.

When we recognize our lesser thoughts for what they are, these thoughts become vulnerable to becoming powerless in our lives. Let us identify the things that we connect to our lack of progress. We make these things powerless through awareness. The tools to triumph over these moments of adversity in our lives have been freely given to us. What issues have become barriers to your future plans? These things (not freely given) are standing between you and what you desire (note that everything on this list will not be tied to your identity).

Nothing in the universe is powerful enough to stop the power of what you believe in. This means that your belief system (which is free) is the source to your past, current, and future state. Everything that has made your life into what it is today has been freely given to you. Evidence supports this truth because no one can make you believe something; you have complete control over this. What you believe to be true has power and authority to impact your life in accordance to your beliefs.

Think of the elements that separate those who are respected as great from others. The defining factor will always come down to what has been freely given to us by the Formless Intelligence. At the root of any great person is proper use of time. No one has an advantage or disadvantage when it comes to time; the same amount is given to all. Look at self discipline. Can one have more access to it than someone else, based on any factor that could be named? No, they cannot! Or take perseverance, integrity, or passion. Anything needed to achieve greatness is available to every man and woman, free of charge. Use what has been given to generate A Powerful mindshift.

CHAPTER 5
SUMMARY

As we have discovered, we are a three part being: soul, mind, and body. Your soul is greater than the body, and your mind is controlled by the stronger of the two elements. If the lesser part of you (the flesh) is stronger, you will take on things from your environment and allow what is seen and heard to be interpreted by the mind. These things make up who you are.

The greater part of you is your soul, connected to the Formless Intelligence. Your greater self cannot have control without complete conscious thought. This means that what is consumed by the body must be closely monitored. Even when a person's environment or circumstances are not desirable, the greater self remains unimpacted. This is because it does not allow what is seen to impact what could be. You are greater than anything that has, can, or will happen to you.

This is a beautiful part of the evolution. The lesser will not give way to the greater without a fight, which is why it needs your body to become addicted to something. In these times, people understand that there is a way that seems to be right, but their greater self reminds them of a way that is better. The ability to act upon what is better depends on the strength of the soul and body. Imagine your greater self and lesser self in an arm wrestling contest. Who would win? If your lesser self wins the match, it is only because you have neglected what is available to you, free of charge.

Using what is free is so simple that it is extremely difficult to execute. This is because it has become part of our human nature to devalue things that are formless and free, even though our livelihood depends on them. This is what makes life fair. Through proper use of what is freely given, the trajectory of your life can change for the better. Use the gift of your purpose, fingerprint, time, and other abstracts provided by the Formless Intelligence in order to impact your life in a way you did not believe to be possible.

6

WHAT'S AT STAKE

"You are greater, so use what is greater to lead the lesser so that your flesh can be used to live out the purpose of something greater than itself."

-LaDrew Murrell-

What is Good and What is Evil

Do not misunderstand the context of what is at stake because what is good does not depend what is evil in order to become good again. What is good, is good all by itself. But what is evil needs what is good so that it to may become good or continue to oppose what is good. This is how the Formless Intelligence is: we need it but it does not need us. We did not align the universe, and we are not responsible for the sustainability of our earth. In spite of this, we continue to use its resources, and it sustains itself for us. However, what is good prefers us and needs us in order to free ourselves from the bondage of evil. Evidence can be shown through the ocean and the land which is lesser in mass and hierarchy. The ocean could sustain itself without the land being present, but the land without the water would be no more; the lesser is totally dependent on the greater. So good and evil follows the same principle. What is good could live independently from what is evil, but what is evil can only be present if it has something to oppose. Good is greater than evil.

I say these things for our understanding so that we do not misinterpret the ways of the formless world. The Formless Intelligence cannot be compared to form, but we can understand formless principles by natural laws. There is no greater natural law to explain the greater versus lesser contrast than that of the sun and moon. You can have too much of the sun but you cannot have too much of what is good. In this example, if what is greater (the sun) dominates the lesser, the result would be the Sahara Desert here on earth, and if what is lesser (the moon) dominates what is greater, the result would be Antarctica. Neither of these conditions are desirable for mankind.

No one can have too much of the greater presence of their soul, or too much connection with the Formless Intelligence. This could only positively impact form on earth. This is because the Formless Intelligence is good and not evil. A person does not have to agree with the thinking of a greater and lesser presence within themselves in order for it to be present. We can all feel when something is wrong or if we are involved in a wrong action, because we receive a signal from our higher government that seeks to live by right doing. This is the part of us that is aligned with the good in the universe. Although we may override the more respectable action and do what pleases ourselves, the soul gives us ability to take the narrow path if we choose. Choosing not to adhere to the greater good results in the evil actions, creating a consciousness that stores these actions in the memory bank. This makes them impossible to forget and more likely to be repeated. These would be the parts of your life that no other person knows about, except for you. The memory of these poor choices you will have to live with forever, and that is a heavy penalty to pay.

Take what is best for you as things that we do not prefer naturally in our bodies, such as working out. Fit or not, everyone has health goals to improve themselves. Now, the body dreads the action until it is made a habit, and even then, it is difficult to persuade the flesh to improve itself by weight training and cardio training. This is because the flesh prefers what is evil. These things stimulate the flesh in ways nothing else can; it feels good, which becomes a feeling that the flesh seeks over and over again. If you were given the desires of your flesh with unlimited resources and were freed from consequences, your thoughts would be predictable and selfish. If I were to guess, every person's wishes would revolve around having: perfect looks, amazing physique, perfect height, unlimited money, a kingdom, cars, a mate (or two, or more), amazing food, wine and spirits, no job, beaches, mountains, perfect weather conditions, and friends and family to enjoy it with. These things are self-seeking as the flesh seeks to please itself first, which is the opposite of sustaining a relationship with your inner self or anyone else. What is good, which is your soul, would put itself second to the needs of others. This list would not be as predictable because it would depend on the needs of your community and the world during the time you occupied it. For example, during my time on earth, we need an abundance of peace, love, compassion for others, and a lot less of materialism which is where society forces you to receive your identity. Today we are almost forced to become one-dimensional due to materialism and self-centeredness. These formless measures could change humanity in a positive way but would be contrary to the flesh because it places others needs ahead or equal to your own.

As long as you cannot resist your flesh, evil will rule over you in a way that will not allow you to make the better or best choice. This is the most difficult task on earth: resisting your flesh, its desires, and changing your mind to access something greater. Unfortunately, what is greater is not always perceived that way by mankind. What is greater is almost likely to oppose our nature.

War for the Mind

The concept of greater versus lesser is a competition to win over the mind, which holds the power of thought. It is in our best interest to understand that the thoughts within our mind produce what is seen by the eye. What is seen by the eye, the mind perceives again as thought. A mindshift can change your world as you know it; the only charge is that you must recognize your thoughts when they happen. If you do not accept your current reality, you must see differently in order to think differently. Not believing in this truth does not take away the law. The mind will manifest itself no matter what you believe. Your subconscious thoughts are supported by the heart, which is the formula which creates what you see in form because of the subconscious belief. Therefore, your conscious thoughts must become a part of your subconscious thinking in order to produce its equivalent in form. So, just as the goodness of the Formless Intelligence does not depend on you being good, our only chance to become whole is understanding our Source. We must work to become more like it and less like the flesh. Being governed by the soul allows your mind to be restored and your body to embrace self-discipline because the strength of the soul is greater than the desires of the body.

The mind is literally being pulled in two different directions. The difficulty within the system is that what is form has the authority to override what is formless. This is "free will" in the fullness of its effect. For example, you may want to lose weight and incorporate healthier life habits, but your flesh overrides the desires of the formless soul and does what is self-pleasing. This makes it extremely difficult to engage your higher self into who you are. For the higher self to have authority, it must rule over your use of free will. The fact that no one can make you change your mind is a critical factor. You must become convicted in wanting better for yourself in all areas of life. Without deep conviction, your flesh will win the battle every time. Think of a soldier protecting your country, and although you do not know them or that they even exist, their conviction to protect their country is stronger than their flesh wanting to live for itself. This person would die for you and they do not know you, or whether you are good, bad, or deserving of someone dying for you. However, their conviction dictates the thoughts in their mind which makes up the reality of their life. Regardless of your actions (good or bad) or regardless of how many times their body told them to quit or give up, they stay true to the belief in their mind and heart. Many soldiers have sacrificed their life so that you can live in peace today.

So how does your soul thrive when it can be overridden by your flesh? How can one win when the system gives your addiction and impure desires easier access to what it wants than the soul has access to establishing what its desires are? The answer is simple: mind training. Just as physical training is of value, training mentally is of even greater value because it is formless. There are no limits to what you can think of in the mind. Can you resist what the flesh wants and do what the soul desires? The answer is simple: Are you the person that your New Year's resolution describes? If you are, once you have met those goals, have you created even higher heights to achieve? No matter what your answer is, you must begin your mental regimen. This is how you will win the war for your mind.

Your mental regimen starts with your thinking. Are you in constant thought about your own thoughts so that you are aware of what you are thinking at all times? In education, we call this metacognition, which can simply be defined as thinking about your thinking. For example, we all fear something, and no matter what age you are, there are concerns that place doubt in your mind about your future or even your day. Your today can also be ruined because of your yesterday, last week, last month, or last year. The beginning of formless training starts with recognizing these fears when they enter your mind and replacing it with the positive outcome inside of that same fear.

A young child may fear being accepted at school. A young adult may fear never finding the correct mate to marry. An adult may stress about paying bills or finding a suitable job. An older person may begin to fear death. When they enter the mind, these thoughts must be recognized and replaced with their equivalent thought in the positive realm. The child should embrace self-acceptance, while the young adult should become one with themselves. The adult should find their fingerprint and work within it, and the elderly should place their hope in the unseen world. Even if your fears are concrete like the family you were born into, your current environment, or your looks and height, you can replace these thoughts with an equal positive thought.

Our mind is impacted by what we see or watch with our eyes, what we hear with our ears, what we say with our mouth, and what we eat. This all impacts how we understand and interpret the information that we receive in form. This limits how we use the formless abstracts of the universe. To keep matters as simple as possible, start your training with thoughts impacted by what you see, have seen, or predict to see. Replace these fears with their positive equivalent, and it will impact what you listen to, say, eat, and spend your time on. Set an alarm to go off hourly so that if negative thoughts have ruled your last hour, you can replace them before they impact the next hour. Do this until metacognition becomes a habit. A key indicator that you are winning the war for the mind is the evaluation of what your time is spent on. At this point, you should spend ample time evaluating your own thoughts.

Think about what your flesh has convinced your mind to think you could not accomplish, and begin to pursue it. Start with thoughts you think throughout the day and how you can keep them aligned with the desires you have for yourself or your family. Do not focus on the fears that you associate with your life. With your time, begin to implement the ideas or action steps it would take to begin your journey. Has your flesh persuaded you not to do the following write a book, love or accept yourself, travel the world, finish school, lose weight, open a bakery, learn how to play an instrument, apologize or forgive a loved one? You fill in the blank here, and get started. A powerful mindshift is waiting on you. Do not let doubt rise in your mind.

The Unknown (How do I Know What is Unknown?)

Here is a trustworthy statement that should be pursued until it is understood: What is unknown does not need to become known in order to exist; it is far greater than what is known, or what will become known. The unknown is far more powerful than things that are known. Since the unknown is greater, it does not have to be discovered in order to exist. What is greater can now be understood, therefore, know that the unknown is more abundant than what can be seen or known. This makes things that are seen a small snippet of what could be. Things that are known manifest through form, while the unknown only reveals itself through time as mankind becomes capable of understanding.

The unknown is like this: The first skyscraper on earth was built in Chicago in 1884-1885 standing at 138 feet. Before this, engineering such a structure was unknown, however, the skyscraper itself has been here since the creation of the world. Mankind was only unaware of its existence until architectural laws were discovered to execute such a task. Since this time, building skyscrapers has become vastly pursued by mankind. In Dubai 2,717 feet marks today's tallest skyscraper in the world, and this only broadens the perspective of what is unknown to man as it relates to skyscrapers of the future. All along, what was greater was present, waiting patiently to become known by mankind. Its existence did not depend on becoming known to man.

We can know the unknown by understanding that the unknown is greater than what is known. You now understand that what is greater by no means relies on what is lesser, therefore, the unknown is all powerful and unlimited. The unknown is formless and never takes form until it becomes known. Some things never take form and remain in the realm of what is unknown to us, which causes anxiety especially when the afterlife is the topic of discussion.

You may ask where do we go after we die on earth? If you can apply the teachings of this chapter, you will understand what is very difficult to explain in a way that you are now willing to accept. When we die, we enter a formless state that is unknown to man. What we know about the unknown is that it is far greater than what is known and does not need what is known in order to function or exist. What is unknown can be revealed through connection with the Formless Intelligence by submission to the greater self. But, if you understand the law, you will know by its principle that the afterlife is far more advanced than life as we currently know it. This formless kingdom will remain unknown to us.

It is known that humans only use 10 to 15 percent of our brain's functional abilities. The unknown 85 to 90 percent is understood to be capable of much greater things than the percentage of the brain that we are using. In medicine, we dedicate time and money to finding cures or ways to improve the body, and a lifetime's worth of studying could be done on one element of the body without mastering its content. The functioning of the human body is not totally known to man, so we divide to conquer as someone studies each part so that we can find ways to slow down the inevitable path of death. When more things become known to us, through time and discovery, we find something else that was once unknown.

Find comfort because unknown aspects of the universe actually prefer to become known to us. Many people already understand the power of a mindshift, and how this formless power creates in form what it meditates on and truly believes in. These are then supported by your subconscious mind and developed into what you see in form. Many people are not aware of its existence, therefore, they become victims of its law and are ruled, marginalized, and eventually become dominated by their flesh and environment.

Looking into the greater part of who we are is very beneficial. What is formless is available to us and accessible to the body under the circumstance that the body must be governed by the greater presence of who you are. It is wise to invest in what is unlimited. Investing in the flesh leaves you subject to what your looks, body, and intellect are capable of. Your soul is what you can feel inside of you, but is difficult to explain; you can hear it without saying a word, and it knows your deepest and darkest secrets. No matter what you believe, you know that there is something there; and this something is the unlimited formless presence of your soul.

Here is something to know about the unknown: Your soul seeks to rule over the body. The difficult part is that many of its benefits do not initially include simple pleasures. The soul is rich in love, peace, faith, goodwill, work ethic, servanthood, self-control, and other things like this. Your lesser self opposes the thought of being governed by such traits because it operates by things that are known and prefers stimulants that feel good to the body. The only way to reach your soul is to seek it. Whether your soul is known or unknown to you, there is more to know. The difficulty is that no one can know your soul for you. The Wright brothers built the first aircraft, and from that, we were given the blueprint to become better flyers. Likewise, people have become masters of their greater self, but only you can mature in the formless inside of you. We are all without excuse and have the ability to accomplish this because the way has been made plain for us through nature and leadership from the past. You can test the strength of the formless presence in your life by taking principles from the greater and battling them against the will of the lesser. Can you defeat addiction? Can you value money less and time more? Shift the mind from depression to peace? Can you do more for others than you do for yourself? Even if you only lack in one of these areas but are competent in the others, your greater self is trampled over by the flesh. Each element seeks total control, so any loss of control leaves the greater or lesser element subject to vulnerability.

To remain ignorant of this is to become subject to negative thoughts which produces a life and body that we pay others to improve or we make resolutions each yeah to fix. To remain ignorant of this is how evolution works to weed out those who are unfit and how poverty is designed to replenish itself. It takes the greater self (our soul) to allow failure and hardships to serve their purpose in our life. A person governed by their greater self would claim that their failures are the greatest resource to their successes. Someone ignorant to the power of a mindshift may quit when failure arrives. To some, it is the fuel that empowers success, and to others, it is their reason to give up. This contrast needs no approval from us in order to work in our life no more than fire needs our permission to be hot. Understanding this will allow you to make an intentional mindshift from the flesh to the soul.

Again, take your profession and your area of expertise and think about how long you have devoted yourself to that specific craft. Even within your craft, there will be an ability to grow as your craft evolves. So, even within what you know best, you still do not know enough. Therefore, understand that whatever is known by you is minimal in comparison to the information that is already known to man. If we are looking at all areas, what we do know is minimal compared to what is known. A dentist is not competent as a physical therapist, the pilot is not competent as a lawyer, and the architect is not competent as a mechanic. With this being the case, it is not wise to become dependent on your understanding of the unknown, the Formless Intelligence, or the makeup of the invisible world. We ourselves do not know all that there is to know about our craft; and furthermore, we do not know all of the things that have become known to man. Knowing the unknown becomes as simple task: The unknown is always greater than the known and will always be greater than what is known by man, until time runs its course. In this statement you can place all of your hope.

Let's discover this image in our minds together as the paradigm of the unknown and known are like this: There is a large-arm balance scale that resembles the ancient scales used long ago. Except this scale was much bigger than the earth. In the sky, a gold beam stretched over the earth and also in the other direction so far that the other scale pan could hardly be seen. It was so far that the gold pan opposite of the earth looked like the twinkling of a small star. To begin, the pans were equal in weight. Then the weight of the earth was measured along with all things known by man. This is the sum of everything seen and unseen with a man-made source. Immediately, the scale pan holding the earth began to out leverage the other scale pan. As the weight of what is known kept increasing, the balance became even more drastic in difference and soon, the weight of what is known was so heavy that the other scale pan was high above the earth as if it had nothing on it to balance the weight of what is known and becoming known. More and more became known, and the distance became greater until the gold that looked like the twinkling of a star disappeared is space. Everyday people would wake up and look into the sky for the other scale pan because the arm beam could still be seen, as the opposite end was still pointing upward.

Things stayed this way for thousands of years, until one day, a messenger was sent from above to inform the people about the unknown. It had turned out that the balance system that we had known was actually opposite to the upside down order of the universe so that the unknown elevated the more things becoming known to mankind. No matter how much became known to man, they would never see the unknown because the weight of it was far greater than the weight of what was known. So much that the mass of the unknown did not change when things became known on earth. As more things became known on earth, the distance between what was known and the unknown increased due to man's inability to handle knowledge with integrity. So what became known was mismanaged and was no benefit to the majority of the population on earth.

So the sum of all things known on earth (which could be seen in form) plus what was known by every living person, plus all things known by anyone that ever lived, was not enough to move the scale one inch. Unfortunately, this did not stop people on earth from trying to know more than the unknown. The messenger from above pleaded with the people to listen to his instructions, but the upside down understanding of the greater could not be comprehended by them. They felt that the more things became known, the closer they would get to seeing the star again. But their knowledge and technological advancements only took them further away from where they intended to go. No one ever saw the other side of the balance scale again.

Remember, what is unknown is still formless. We must not allow what becomes known by us to take us further away from the rest of what is unknown. To understand what is formless, we must begin our training. We must train in the formless like a bodybuilder trains their physique. It takes daily attention that is intentional, scheduled, and focused on different areas to develop the whole self. In this way, your soul and body can work as one, instead of working against one another seeking to have the mind submissive to its desires.

Formless Training

In order to train in the formless realm, you must have a strong investment in yourself. You must become your priority. We all have several reasons why this cannot happen: children, job, bills, spouse, family, parents, or life's many other responsibilities. To train in the formless, you must be connected to the formless source: the Formless Intelligence. If you do not believe in a higher spiritual government, your only option is to train in the realm of form and take a more scientific approach to a formless scenario. In science, you must look at yourself as the source and depend on your skills and good fortune in order to achieve success. Here, success can only be tied to acquiring what the flesh seeks is capable of obtaining. To train in what is known is not the beneficial choice to one working to operate in soul, mind, and body. Training in the formless requires much self-discipline and the incorporation of these non-negotiable practices:

Meditation - If you focus on your breathing, you will feel something that you would never identify throughout the course of a typical day. As you inhale, feel the energy flow through the body all the way from your fingers to your feet. Due to the business of life and the mental demands of the day, the conscious mind does not usually recognize this energy. It is necessary to be still and allow this energy to flow as you consciously connect with it. During this time, your mind will not wonder, but soon, your soul will take the gateway to communicate with you in a way that could not have been achieved any other way. Please do not confuse communication from the greater with communication from the lesser. Anytime you are hearing solutions and ideas, this is from the greater presence. If you are hearing doubt and fear having the final say, you know that the lesser is communicating to you. Through meditation, you are practicing how to shift the mind in a functional way that produces what you want out of life.

You should meditate first thing in the morning in a quiet space with nature sounds through music or no sound at all. This should also be done throughout the day as you go about your normal activities. This keeps your greater self in control of your thoughts. Anytime negativity enters the thought waves, they must be recognized and then removed. Understand that it is predictable that these thoughts will pursue attention from your mind. After you have recognized a negative thought, replace it with the equivalent positive thought in the same area of worry. For example, if you think negatively about waking up in the morning and executing your daily plan, recreate this thought with the positive equivalent of waking up and dominating the day. You may say that you have heard this before or that this does nothing in reality, but I hope that you understand that this is about formless training. You are practicing how to control the mind through the greater self, and this is the skill that will change the condition of your life. Everyone experiences fear and doubt, but successful people do not dwell in these things. As you develop this, clarity will come to you about what you should produce, because you are living in your purpose and controlling your mind. Everyone is charged with the obligation to produce. Being cognizant of what to produce is the difference in your product being pleasing to the Formless Intelligence or distasteful. When you produce through your greater self, intentional thought leads your steps. At this point, your unique fingerprint will connect itself with your new thought patterns. These are the ideas that should be pursued because when conflict presents itself, you can persevere because this work is who you are.

Dieting From Flesh - You should give up something of great value for two weeks at a time, all year long, so every day, the flesh is being denied something that it desires. This forces the lesser to understand that it is not in control and that something greater is. In this case, the lesser function loses power over you, and eventually, it will seek to regain its power less and less because the lesser only seeks to dominate the weak minded individual. The lesser does not fight against a strong will; it only seeks easy victories.

A healthy fitness routine is non-negotiable and should be in every weekly schedule, however this is not enough. Everyone must make physical sacrifices that are challenging to your personal lustful desires. Here are the three areas that gain you the most strength as you train in the formless: dietary pleasure, sexual pleasure, and serving others. For optimal strength, you should be engaged in refusing one of these three areas at all times. If you are able to follow through with your goals in these areas, you will be able to create mindshifts in any area of your life.

- Diet

Giving up alcohol, sweets, meat, soda, carbs, or other desirable foods. These are great ways to connect with the greater presence as you will be constantly aware that you are giving up something you want because you are devoted to shifting your mind to a greater cause. This will only benefit your mind and body in a healthy way and compliment your exercise by producing a physique that is closer to what your goals are for yourself in this area. Keeping two week cycles without cheating on the weekends will truly test the power of the greater versus lesser presence in your life. Challenge yourself as you decide what to give up, and choose what you will replace what is given up with. For example, you may give up soda and replace it with sparkling water.

You must eat, but you do not have to eat everything, and this is evident in the amount of money generated in the health industry. People want to buy their way to the body they want, when you could simply obey your greater self and obtain it naturally, little by little. This area should be exercised all year long, which will turn a diet into a life habit. When you are happy with your body, all aspects of your life receives its due increase.

- Sexual Desires

Married or not, we all have ways to sacrifice. Many are addicted to masturbation and pornography. In marriage, this has no place as it steals the zeal for fiery love and passionate intimacy with your spouse and fills it with desires of variety outside of the relationship. It also replaces a natural act with an unnatural substitute. For single people, it prioritizes the wants of the lesser presence and trains you to feed that appetite instead of the greater presence and its appetite. In either dynamic, you lose, and you allow a positive natural energy to escape your body due to a false connection to a screen. Married couples should work to replace the desire to use pornography with passion towards one another. This would add many benefits to the relationship including a sexual release. Singles could workout to subdue the sensation, or practice their craft with the energy that has not left the body falsely. Relationships can also be improved by replacing sexual affairs with romance and communication so that each partner is receiving attention in other aspects of the union. Just like eating, sex is on our minds constantly, and if we can control our sexual appetite, there is nothing within ourselves that we cannot control. Resisting sexual pleasures are not only difficult but necessary in order to strengthen the greater self.

I understand that this may be difficult to accept, and a single person may question what they should do with all the hormones that get bottled up. The answer is to create something with that energy. You are fulfilling your purpose by taking control of your mind, so take your fingerprint and use it, or develop it for the first time ever. Maybe you have always wanted to play an instrument, but you never learned how; use the time once given to satisfying the lesser and develop your gift with that time. The energy will still be released this way. Couples will find themselves being aroused at the touch of their partner once again as their sexual organs are no longer abused during meaningless and unnatural aims to satisfy their flesh.

- Serving Others

Providing a service requires extreme sacrifice and requires you to completely deny the lesser portion of yourself so that you can give yourself to someone that is in need. This should be done even if you yourself are in need. No matter how busy your life is, you must give your time along with other formless abstracts to others. This could be a parent coaching their child's sports team, volunteering at a nursing home or prison, or serving a nonprofit organization. There are so many programs that allow us to serve for a greater cause, and this exercise creates foundational strength in formless training. Serving is also therapeutic to the soul. You will notice that you will gain much pleasure from serving. Many times, it gives back more to the giver than what you may be attempting to give someone else.

At all points in time, you should be giving something up in at least one of these three areas. For quicker results, practice two areas at the same time all year long. The mindshift will become a way of life and a focal point of each day, allowing you to shift your life into your own desires that will not be overtaken by the desires of the lesser part of who you are. By this time, we notice that the lesser part of us needs close supervision, and it also needs boundaries with barriers that will not be crossed to prevent us from destructive behavior, which ends in negative consequences. Meanwhile, the greater part of ourselves needs no rules or boundaries because the only things it deprives us of are things that are detrimental to our own health and others wellbeing. We should work to allow this to become our conviction.

In education, we always focus on the phrase "hook the learner," and these three categories act as hooks to lure you out of the lowly realm of existence. They are the quickest and most efficient avenues to get you to deny the lesser and give strength to the greater as they "hook" what is appealing and sought after by the flesh. Whether you are financially rich or poor, these areas are effective. Seek to dominate your life in a way that is in contrast with your lesser self. This is similar to how teachers use external motivation to hook the learner, knowing that students would bite if the hook had a reward that pleases the flesh. Life will hook us by turning our needs and natural expressions into outlets to destroy us given permission of the flesh. As it is, our flesh is willing to co-sign and validate self-destructive choices that we attend to make. Instead, train in the formless realm in one or more areas every day so that you might escape the grasp of the pleasures of the flesh.

I am Greater

Take this phrase and begin to live it out. Refuse to give into what you know is not elevating your soul, mind, and body. You are much greater than the temporary fulfillment that your flesh is seeking every hour of every day. Use your mind to shift into the greatness that is waiting for you. Take this into understanding: What is greater does not always feel good to the flesh, and it may not look like the more appealing choice compared to the socially-accepted standard. But, the long term impact that it will have on your life will far outlast the dissolving joy your flesh receives from engaging in lesser actions.

If you follow this path, anticipate criticism because the greater path may seem lesser to those who are not connected to the Formless Intelligence. Understand that those governed by their greater self will become outcasts as the majority are unaware of the frequency that they operate on. We become separated while we are conscious of every thought we think and every move we make. Understand that this way may not look better than those that are governed more loosely; they may have more stuff than you at the present time. But, can anyone even name one benefit of lesser desires and actions, or can anyone find form that will last forever? The actions of the lesser and things it works to obtain may seem more desirable at a glance, however, they were acquired on false and unstable principals that cannot provide an unmovable surface to build your life upon. You are greater than the flesh your soul lives in. Deny it for the greater good of yourself and the world that needs you.

You are greater, so use what is greater to lead the lesser so that your flesh can be used to live out the purpose of something greater than itself. Many people work a lifetime to own something, but you own your body, and it has no other choice than to work for what is greater than itself. Now the lesser part of yourself can live on formless principles which creates harmony and unity between your greater and lesser self. Soon enough, there will be no more war for the mind because the lesser will submit to the will of the greater once the formless things of the world begin to become more visible.

CHAPTER 6
SUMMARY

- Can you: see with your eyes who you really are, and become what you were destined to be? No matter what you currently see, have seen, or predict to see, the formless you is greater and cannot be manipulated or diminished by physical circumstances.
- Can you: hear with your ears truth and words of wisdom, and apply them to your life so that you will stop fearing the hardships that are guaranteed to come? Does the adversity and failure that enters your life aide in the process of your development, or pacify your existence in a false realm of who you should be? If you can hear these words, know that hardships are supposed to come, and they serve the purpose of bettering you and teaching you lessons that could not have been learned any other way.
- Can you: believe in your heart that you can? Can you believe that you are great so that your actions and

speech will confirm it? You will only say what you hold true in your heart. Only fools do not believe in themselves.
- Can you: rise in your mind so that you can become whole (3/3) and see to it that your mind will manifest your thoughts through form in the way you chose.

Understanding these things do not make them any easier to accept. However, there is much power in believing in the unknown and trusting that there is a plan in place for your life that means you well. Place your confidence in the fact that more will be unknown by you than what is known by you. This is the source for humility, and this humbleness keeps your dependance towards the Formless Intelligence.

Train in a way that increases the strength of your greater self so that the body is always doing without something that it desires. Use what is greater to impact the lesser so that you will have an influence on your body that will benefit you and those within your sphere of influence.

Submit to the Greater Self.

BECOME THE SOLUTION

"The solution is to see the formless solution."
-LaDrew Murrell-

The solution can only happen in the realm of your greater self because thinking in this way requires an extreme amount of self-discipline. In this realm, you take what used to make you the victim of circumstance and use it to promote ideas for solutions to your adversities. Solutions in the greater self oppose victimhood because no solution can ever be found in the victim mindset. Without mastery over the lesser (which is your flesh) you cannot move on to becoming the solution to your adversities. Understand that your adversities are only here to serve the purpose of bringing to your attention solutions to your own inefficiencies. This requires you to be able to view problems in the light that makes them possibilities. The greater self will ask, "What new possibilities is this problem showing me? What am I lacking that is causing this conflict?" While the lesser self would respond," Here we go again. Why does this always have to happen to me? I wonder what else will go wrong."

In solution-thinking, nothing is definite, not even success. Everything is looked at under a lens that understands the temporary state of form and senses. A solution mindset also understands that new solutions only bring about more opportunities for new "problems". When governed by your greater self, problems and adversity are only indicators of where growth can occur. Without this critical information, growth would not be possible in places where conflict does not show up. A wise person knows that we need the system to work this way because there would be no way to find where we need growth unless conflict is present.

Becoming the solution is like this: There was a teacher who had a student that was capable of excelling academically and was held in high esteem by his peers. But towards the end of each week, the student would become disruptive in class or come into class and refuse to do his work. The teacher tried to bribe the fine athlete with his eligibility status in order to keep him in line. Seeing that it did not work, the teacher knew that this student was dealing with a problem that was bigger than the sports he played. The teacher wondered what need was not being met somewhere else in the student's life, so the teacher set out to find the missing link. The teacher noticed that the beginning of the week always started off great, so they held the student back after school on Mondays to help him get caught up with his work. Many weeks later, the teacher gained his trust and used their bond to locate the problems that were visible. The teacher said to the student, "I notice on Mondays and Tuesdays you are very energetic and well behaved. But, by the middle of the week you come to school sluggish, you are disruptive in class, and you refuse to get your work done. What goes on between Monday and Wednesday in your life that causes this to happen?" The student explained, "Well, on Saturday and Sunday, I get to see my parents on this thing called a supervised visit, and I feel really good inside. But as the week goes on, I start missing them and want to see them again, so I act out in hopes that my foster parents will kick me out and send me back home to my real family." The teacher used what could be seen (the disruptive behavior) as a means to finding a solution that was formless in every sense. A solution was found right in the middle of the conflict. The behavior of the student provided conflict within the classroom structure, disrupting the norms established for learning, which was the indicator that a problem did exist. If the same student came in sat quietly and was compliant with all of the structures for the classroom, no conflict would have been provided to know that any issues were at hand. Since the teacher was thinking through their greater self, what had been perceived by many other teachers as "the problem kid" provided a certain teacher a way to know something was missing. The conflict became the means to the solution. They went on meeting after school and journaled his feelings so he could share his hopes and fears with his parents when they met on the weekends. As the year went on, his parents lost custody to the state, but the young man realized that he could not allow the irresponsibility of his parents affect his future, and he went on graduating at the top of his class and credited his success to his middle school teacher.

To become the solution, you must use this finding: It is predictable that adversities will come in everyone's life, but only in areas that we are not efficient enough in. Using this knowledge, look forward to the problems to come because, without them, you would not know where growth actions were needed in your life. Know that these types of problems only come in areas that could use better management in our lives.

The Aware Thinker

A thinker that is aware is constantly evaluating their own thoughts. If a person has road rage, when they enter that rage, they become aware of their thoughts and what caused them. The aware thinker can escape the powerful grasp of anger by making the circumstance that causes this irritation powerless, simply by recognizing it immediately. This is called a controlled mindshift. Opportunities such as this present itself to us all day long, but you must be constantly aware in order to overcome these poorly manufactured emotions and thoughts. The aware thinker still gets angry, but in that anger they are able to identify the fact that there is an imbalance about themselves. Then, they shift their mind out of that space inside of that same angry moment. An aware thinker has solutions to the things around them that spark negative thoughts or emotions. For example, an aware thinker with road rage would leave their house thirty minutes earlier, so they do not feel rushed in traffic. This is because they understand that everyone's use of the knowledge of the road rules and the invisible barriers will differ from person to person, causing opportunities for road rage during their commute each day. So leaving early and listening to their favorite podcast in the car is a solution that an aware thinker would use in this instance.

The aware thinker does not only recognize this in themselves but also in the people that they encounter. This does not make them judgmental or critical of others, but it helps them consider another point of view without taking actions from others as personal attacks. You only get to this space by mastering the principles of the previous chapters because only conscious mindshifts can keep you in the realm of constant awareness. Here, you are able analyze your own thoughts and reactions and immediately identify whether you were acting from your greater or lesser presence. When you are in the state of an aware thinking, it allows you to be able to rest. This is because the greater action was taken by you all day long, and your time for mental relaxation is not drowned in all of the conflict that you experienced throughout the day. This gives the mind no power to work against itself due to the mastery of mindshifts. The aware thinker can control their thoughts in a way that allows them to stay in a state of meditation. When you fall asleep in this state, your mind is not dominated by your lesser thoughts that only revolve around form. Remember that all form is disintegrating and will one day be no more, which is why it should not be held onto in an unchanging light. So do not give form more value that it is actually worth. Become an aware thinker that mindshifts out of problematic thoughts seconds after they enter the conscious or subconscious realm of the mind.

The aware thinker knows that adversity and resistance in life are steps; the more of it you have, the higher you can go; and without them, it is impossible to elevate to higher ground. This powerful mindshift allows you to see everything from multiple perspectives unimpacted by emotions. It allows you to hear things with the understanding that there is more to it than what can be seen by the eye. By now, you know that what is unseen has a far greater impact on things than what can be seen. Things that can be seen are only small expressions of the unseen world that is continually in our midst. This is the founding principle that the motor vehicle companies thrive upon, as new editions of each car model comes out each year. No matter what year your car is, at one point, it was brand new. And even if you bought your car today, a year from now it will be old news. This is because there is an unseen idea that is waiting to be revealed. People wait in anticipation of the unseen, until the day that it will become seen. And because it is form, shortly after the revelation of the new thing, it will become old and unsatisfying to the one that once held the car in high esteem. By now, you know that the unseen is waiting in anticipation to be discovered by you.

Unlikely to Find Solutions

There are many things in the sequence of life that seem constant, but nothing of form can be constant. This is the number one approach used to keep us affiliated with victim thinking. Our environment, whether good, bad, or mediocre cannot keep us from becoming great. As long as we live, we will become wherever our mindshifts to; so it is in our best interest to live in a state of conscious thought always. Even the most concrete of situations cannot stay the same. It must change everyday just as time must pass second by second. A person's environment by no means can affect what is inside of them. Their fingerprint will stay the same, unimpacted by their physical location.

It is a good thing for you to feel like there are literally no solutions to what you are battling. Otherwise, you would not find how powerful continual mindshifts can be. When a situation that is not desired presents itself, like a disease or sickness, constant mindshifts can be used to combat the state of your mental thinking. But, like getting in shape physically or growing fruits and vegetables, it takes time to see the progress of the mindshift. And even once you begin these shifts, it takes time for these subconscious and conscious thoughts to mature and become form. The harsh reality is that most of the time, whatever we are experiencing, we are only getting the equal consequence of our past actions, or the actions of our parents or ancestors. However, think of this: What good is it to point blame somewhere just because a consequence is not desired. Unfavorable situations deserve new ways of thinking, and in this mindshift, your circumstance does not impact your way of thinking one way or the other. Now we have the understanding that no situation is permanent whether it is desirable or undesirable.

This way, you can experience thoughts and emotions of the lesser realm at a surface level; and in the same, experience thoughts and emotions of the greater realm in a reflective state. When something makes you happy, you understand that you will only feel that way about it for a moment. So you chose to enjoy that feeling while it lasts by being present in that moment, but at some point soon, that feeling will subside, and likewise with unhappy feelings. You are not grounded in that feeling, and your thoughts toward yourself do not change with the situation due to the predictability of the laws of form and the awareness of your own thoughts. A lawyer may feel happy about passing the Bar Exam, but an understanding that your goal of practicing law has just begun follows that emotion. The ultimate self understands that the real opportunities lie ahead, which will be made up of many successes and failures. These can now be called awakening opportunities.

The mindshift is not magic or a miracle that defeats your adversity in the way you would choose to defeat it. So you may remain sick, or your child may never return to your arms, but it gives your mind the freedom to express its most natural thoughts: thoughts that are reflective to the situations in life and not reactive to what happens to you. In everyone, these natural thoughts are alike, just like our purpose is. These natural thoughts are health, happiness, and financial freedom. When circumstances oppose these desires, especially in ways that there seem to be no likely solution, your ability to mindshift in the moment is the solution to your hardship.

Seeing Solutions

Through the laws of nature, we can understand how critical environment is for an element to grow and progress. In order to see solutions in ordinary places, your eyes must see past the environment of the circumstances that you are in. This can only be done if you are viewing it through the lens of your greater self and not your flesh. We have all experienced situations that seem to be concrete: Your earnings are just enough to get you by, and you live paycheck to paycheck. But an unexpected expense comes, and it is mathematically impossible for you to keep things balanced. You do not anticipate getting a promotion, and you have expensed all other resources to help you financially. There is **no way** to pay the bills and move forward with life. This is a very common stress that most can relate to. Unfortunately, many can also relate to this common reaction. If what you see is through the lesser lens, you will lack solutions.

Seeing solutions has everything to do with seeing around the issue at hand. Practice having a 360 perspective rather than viewing your problems face to face. As you know, you yourself are not one-dimensional but you are soul, mind, and body. In the same way, your approach to becoming solution-oriented must involve these three realms, and in that order. When we are dealing with unwanted adversities, an understanding must take place; any problem you face is a result of your own inefficiencies. How you have dealt with what life has presented to you as conflict that has shown up in the way of form? In your environment, if you do not like what you see, you likely only saw things from your lesser lens, which will only allow you to view life as 1/3 or 2/3 of yourself but never whole.

In my experiences as a high school football coach, the lens that you view the game from held a significant impact on my understanding of seeing solutions. Seeing solutions became more evident to me as my roles changed from position coach to coordinator and then head coach. When I was on the sideline, even as an expert in my knowledge of football, my view of the game was extremely limited, and at best I was operating as 2/3 of myself. To my demise, my flesh and emotions were right next to the action. I was being provoked by the elements of the game, officials, score, opponent, and all the more. It wasn't until I moved up to the press box as a coordinator that I saw things differently and was able to remove my emotions from my thinking. I was able to become whole in this atmosphere because who I was and my emotional reactions did not get in the way of reflective thought from my greater government. The press box on a football field is like viewing a problem from a 360 perspective. From the pressbox you can see absolutely everything, and with technology, your iPad could show you the endzone view or a replay in real time. This is equivalent to a controlled mindshift. Seeing things from the press box with an endzone view gave very different perspectives to problems because the only lens you are seeing through is a greater lens which recognized all of the difficulties of the game, but did not hold onto the conflict as a problem. Instead, problems could be used to find new solutions. Instead of seeing from the lesser which would say, "They are bigger, stronger, and more talented than our team." The greater lens kept me focused on solutions because the view kept me in the realm of mindshifts towards solutions. I still got angry, frustrated, felt defeated, puzzled at what to do next, upset with officials, and all the more. However, in view through the greater lens, none of these thoughts or emotions were dwelled upon or considered final. I learned that in order to see solutions, I had to view the game through the proper lens, and if what I was viewing was only the things that could be seen at eye level, the solution would often fail. You must see the solution from the inside of yourself and from a 360 view.

You give yourself no chance to see solutions from the lesser lens, so the power is in knowing what lens you are viewing from. This way, your situation becomes subject to your choices rather than a false state of uncontrollable circumstances. If I chose to come out of the press box and coach from the sidelines, I knew exactly what I was giving up and what lens I would view the game from, which would automatically limit my effectiveness as a coach. I could still see solutions from this view, but emotions, the weather elements, the size and athletic ability of the other team may become too overwhelming for my lesser self to see past, due to my limited view. Sure, your monthly earning may be less than what your bills are, but have you evaluated your management of the resources you earn and how you have prioritized your spending? Your conflict could be a direct reflection of the choices you have made. Accepting responsibility for actions made through the lesser self is not always easy. But there is still a solution in this hardship that we all face, so do not view problems from the sideline and point out the obvious. You are overwhelmed by the bills that you have coming in, but even a kid in elementary school knows greater than and less than differences between two numbers. The question is, what formless solutions can be found and used to counter against this tough situation? Look at any sport. When an inferior team beats a team with better athletes, it is simply because the organization chose to look at the circumstance through their greater lens, which is the only lens that shows us that nothing of form is concrete. It must change and adapt to your thought.

The solution is to see the formless solution. Formless solutions quickly turn into form once you take action to the thought. However, you must make the thought known by the conscious mind and put into action what was once formless. This can be as simple as an idea. If your bills are too great, look into your job and notice if you are working inside of your fingerprint. If you are, use your free time to become better at your craft by studying and practicing more. You will develop skill, which will put you in higher demand, resulting in more income. If you are working a job that is not within your fingerprint, use your free time to begin working on developing the fingerprint inside of you. When you are working with what is inside of you, your skill will be in demand, and others will pay you for what you have that no one else can produce. Working within your fingerprint is like this: A certain hairdresser is preferred by her customers so much that no matter what salon she moves to, or how much she charges, or how far out, she is booked. Her clients will find a way to use her for her services. What is on the inside of that hairdresser cannot be reproduced by anyone else, which makes her gift something that is demanded no matter where she goes. Or again working within your fingerprint is like this: An employee looks into all of the areas of their job that people complain about, which is creating a lack of investment in the company. Furthermore, it results in poor productivity compared to the competition. The employee then sits down to see the formless solutions to these issues and presents their ideas to the management team. She is later promoted within the company with an increase of salary that allows her to cancel out her financial debts.

If you neglect this teaching, you will fall over and over again, because at some point you will fall down in life. The means that brings you back to your feet is the difference. Do you fight against yourself as you make it to your feet, expecting to never fall again? Or do you get up by way of mindshifts, knowing that you will fall again but vow not to fall the in same way? The good news is that either lens is available to you and both are free. You can go from the lesser lens to the greater lens, or from being on the field to going up to the press box within a matter of a mindshift. In either view, your mind will shift, even if you do not know it. Therefore, the value is being aware of the shift within your mind so you will shift towards solutions. The lesser lens will only focus on abstracts of form that seem concrete, forcing your mind to shift to victimhood when any resistance comes your way. This way, you may become intimidated by your bills, or the size of your opponent, their speed, or even blame your environment, or the officials of the game. But in no way will this lesser lens lead you to solution-oriented thought. When you use your mindshift to elevate what you see, you are an aware thinker that observes the thoughts that you think. And when issues arise, you see them from a lens where many solutions are evaluated, and a certain one is selected as the solution to the adversity at hand. Even when that does not work, you are equipped to find another way.

When you are able to use your mindshifts in ways that are controlled by your greater self and not by the situation you are in, you are able to understand that everything and everyone is flawed. This will change how you deal with others. Their impact on what you are going through will become minimal because you are in control of your own life. Here is a fact that should be noted: Divorce sucks. But you should not blame your ex-spouse for everything post-divorce. Should the kids should blame their parents for their rocky upbringing due to lack of consistency in their lives? In situations like these, where emotions run high and court orders seem concrete, your mind must shift to seeing solutions, or else you will become the victim of impossible seeming circumstances. What is seen as unlikely to find solutions acts as fuel to the negative thoughts in a person's mind. Instead, see solutions in the worst of circumstances.

Constant Mindshifts

In the solution realm, which is dominated by your greater self, you must learn to shift your thoughts continually throughout the day. This takes constant practice because you can never master it. Every day, life looks for an advantage to get the best of you, and if you are not aware of the lens you are using, you will become subject to lesser responses to both success and failure. This in itself is a workout because it takes extreme self-discipline to monitor your every thought and where that thought is coming from. To be able to do this is like running a marathon because for twenty-four hours, your mind is surrounded by form stuff: things to do, bills to pay, health concerns, financial problems, homework, relationship problems, deadlines to meet, and goals for the future. This will even interrupt your sleep, so you must remain on guard for all twenty-four hours. Constant mindshifts can only be done by continuous training, like a runner training for a marathon.

Acts that we have committed, whether known by others or not, will always remain in our own memory. This means that we have created a lifelong job for ourselves due to the mindshifts that will need to occur because of these choices. These past actions or future fears may even creep into your dreams, which makes the stakes for a constant mindshift even higher. This is why we must fulfill our purpose and take every thought that we think and put it under the surveillance of our greater self. This is the only way to master constant mindshifts.

Think of your professional goals: graduate school, starting a business, working towards a promotion. Think of your health goals: losing weight, gaining mass, getting lean, gaining more speed or agility. If you have not reached them, it is only because you have not mastered the ability to monitor every thought in a way that will allow the mind to shift towards solutions. You cannot accomplish these difficult things without mastery of mindshifts because at the gateway of any great accomplishment is an abundance of adversity, and if you see this adversity in the view of "sideline" instead of the "press box" view, you will never overcome the things that seem impossible. So we must train to constantly shift our mind to the formless realm that is greater.

An hour should not go by where you have not evaluated your thoughts and the responses that you have had to things going on in the past hour of your life. In this way, you can monitor the lens you are viewing the situation from. We have all heard that hindsight is 20/20, but it does not take years, months, days, or hours to see from a different perspective. It only takes a mindshift, which can happen in a moment in time. In this way, we can improve from hour to hour and not year to year. Think to yourself: Did my thoughts from that last hour stem from my emotions and the elements of form that make up the environment that my problems come from? If you did a poor job of taking in information from adversity, it is no big deal, as long as you correct it within an hour. You can still come to solutions in the same day by way of a mindshift, which only takes seconds.

There are programs to train people to go from their couch to running a marathon. This program will train you to go from unevaluated thought patterns to evaluating every thought as it enters the mind, pairing the subconscious mind with your conscious thoughts. The first part of the exercise is giving up something of lesser value that takes up your time and adding this into your calendar from chapter 1.

<u>Week 1</u>

Set an alarm on your phone to alert you at 4 p.m. When that alarm goes off, bring to the front of your mind the things throughout the day that have not gone well for you, big or small. Set another alarm for a time before you know you will go to bed, let's say 9:30 p.m. During this time, start exploring solutions to one of the things that did not go as planned. Even if the thing that comes to your mind was resolved by a solution that you used in the moment, reflect and think of a better solution that could have been used in that same moment.

Do this exercise every day during the first week.

<u>Week 2</u>

Continue the practice from week one, and incorporate this mind exercise into your down time for fifteen to thirty minutes, twice per week. I would recommend doing this in a quiet place in your home that is comfortable, and if that is not possible, this can be done during a commute to work, cleaning, during dinner, or any other activity where you will have about a half an hour to yourself.

Meditate on an idea or dream that you have for yourself. Envision yourself in this role and doing what you are passionate about. Go through what it would take for you to get to this point: the work you would have to put in, or the risks you would have to take in order to fulfill this dream of yours. As you meditate, do not allow any other thoughts to enter your mind, and when distractions come, eliminate them by shifting your mind back towards your vision.

Incorporate this exercise twice per week during the second week while continuing the exercise from week 1.

Week 3

Continue your meditative practice twice per week, for fifteen to thirty minutes at a time along with the week one regimen. In addition to these two things, start using the slogan, "Now that's the power of a mindshift!" anytime throughout the day when you recognize that you have shifted a rise in your mind that has allowed you to use your greater lens. Say to yourself out loud or in your head, "Now that's the power of a mindshift!" This is a way to congratulate yourself as you respond in ways outside of the lesser view of things that happen throughout the day.

Week 4

This is the first activity that takes self-discipline in form: journaling. Make a list of things that usually cause you to "react" through the lesser scope more times than not. This way, you can bring to the front of your mind the things that cause you stumble throughout the day. After each obstacle, write the necessary mindshift followed by the proper action so you develop a game plan when the situation presents itself as you predict that it will. Each day will give you the opportunity to practice these mindshifts, and you should select things that you know will occur within a typical day for you. These are calculated mindshifts, and practice makes perfect.

You have now brought to the forefront of the mind your desire to shift your mind to the greater lens and view life from this perspective. You should now have a foundation set to continue this progression naturally. If you find yourself struggling, repeat step four and calculate responses in places that cause you to trip up until you can recognize them naturally in the heat of the moment.

Use figure 1 to understand this process. Use figure 2 to engage this practice:

Antagonist	Mindshift	Action	Result
Bills	Decide to control finances	Make a spreadsheet for expenses and meal prep lunch	Save $200 per month by not eating out and buying snacks during working hours
Job	Decide to increase my value by reading	Replace TV time with reading and limit/ delete 50 percent of social media apps	More time to use on mind growth activities to enhance value
Anxiety	Decide not to accept anxiety as an aspect of who you are	Focus on what can be controlled and provide solutions to the problems faced	Mind will shift to the positive equivalent of the situation that leads to anxiety
Fatigue	Decide to incorporate self-discipline into diet and life habits	Drink one gallon of water per day and create a bedtime routine that does not change M-F	More energy throughout the day

Figure 2 Use this diagram to discover where calculated mindshifts can occur within your life.

Antagonist	Mindshift	Action	Result

CHAPTER 7
SUMMARY

If solutions are a stumbling block for you, the area that is impacted most in being solution-oriented is seeing the inside of yourself. To be able to see here, you must have access to the greater lens which drives purpose. Your purpose is what drives action and keeps your character in line. Your greater self must be stronger than the lesser self, and since they are in conflict each day, it takes intentional and strategic planning to defeat the lesser: minute by minute, day by day, month by month, and year by year.

Since this formula is a hierarchy, it is impossible to meet solutions without living as the ultimate self and seeing everything through the greater lens. In this way, it follows the laws of the physical body; if you are in good physical shape, you must work every day to maintain progress and work even harder to improve it, or else you will lose what was gained. So physically, you are cognizant of what you take into your body. In the same way, you must train the greater self to become your ultimate self. And when you arrive, you must work to maintain progress, or work even harder to become better.

The most beneficial solution is in the greater self because it does not harm others, while solutions in the lesser may have a negative impact on someone else, although the situation may have taken a turn for the better for you individually. True solutions are harmonious with the Formless Intelligence that thrives on principals such as love, peace, patience, faith, self-discipline, selflessness, empathy, and the like. Only the aware thinker can manipulate their surroundings in a way that will produce these attributes because sacrifice opposes the lesser self, and the most beneficial solutions will take sacrifice. Through constant mindshifts, you can accomplish this.

Constant mindshifts are the source of solutions. Use the diagram shown in week four's progression to aid you in making calculated mindshifts until these mindshifts become recognized by the subconscious mind and happen automatically.

8

GOOD - BETTER - BEST

"Money only reciprocates the value of a person's values."

-LaDrew Murrell-

20/20

You have heard people say that hindsight is 20/20, but what if you did not have to wait for time to show you a new direction in the moment direction is needed? This happens through viewing things through your greater lens that allows you to see solutions through a mindshift. This system monitors your own thought process and corrects your pattern of thoughts if you are not seeing with your greater eye. In seeking perfect vision through your greater eye, there are physical things that show you in form that you are not on course, allowing you to take corrective action by a mindshift, and actions that follow are directed by that mindshift. For example, if you react out of annoyance or anger to your spouse, child, parent, friend, or coworker that does something you do not like, you will notice that if you do not shift out of that emotion or recognize that you are in it, the situation will fuel and ignite your anger or annoyance and theirs also. This will elevate and cause unwanted friction as you blindly respond out of your lesser lens and act in a way that is not concerned about seeing the solution in the issue at hand.

It takes two people viewing from the greater lens to exercise the learning of truth through source. Having 20/20 vision through your greater lens will require you to identify the source in all things that you encounter. This is powerful because it provides a foundation for understanding. Is this source form and from the maker of a man? A peaceful disagreement might be the best and most realistic solution. This can only happen if all parties understand this truth and see through their greater lens, which will allow you to understand the factors of the other person's feelings that contradict your feelings over the same issue. Or is the source the Formless Intelligence? If so, we understand that we are all flawed as we pursue our ultimate self, and our understanding of the Formless Intelligence is always at a different level than someone else's. However, the common ground is found in what we should put our hope in; and that is in what is unknown. We now know that the unknown is, and has always, been greater than what has been known, or has become known. As you see yourself and others through this greater lens, you understand that everyone is at a different level of understanding things, and nothing has to be taken personal because responses are only "perspectives" from what we have experienced in life or what we have allowed life to teach us. It is not necessary to fight or argue for the sake of things when the source comes from the Formless Intelligence. Often times, it is better to just say, "I don't know," because many things are not known, so there is no shame in that. Anything that is not made or manipulated by the power of mankind should be seen through your greater lens to reduce your struggle with it. This is the lens that can see the inside of what you are looking at.

The information retrieved from what you see should come from both the soul and the flesh. Giving equal balance from what is seen by you aids us as we make sense of the visible and invisible world around us. This allows you to process through your mind after the information has been sifted through by your soul and your senses, creating a wise outlook on all matters that are seen.

The Eye Test

Just like the eye test that we have all taken, you must test your vision frequently. As you covered one eye during the eye test, the giant letter at the top of the chart that everyone gets correct is equivalent to obvious reactions through your lesser self. It's like taking the easy way out or the common reaction to a thing:

If you have a spouse, children, siblings, or parents, they will provide you with a daily eye test. This can be accomplished through normal daily responsibilities. Allow these moments to become learning opportunities in which you can monitor your reactions. These reactions will show you the lens you are viewing from. A child or teenager can also monitor their reactions by how they respond to their parents, coaches, and teachers to see how they are viewing situations. As this becomes habit, you will notice your reactions immediately. This will minimize the many things you had to previously learn through hindsight. Many times, you will come to realize that your responses and reactions only have in mind your desires, or a predetermined end to a situation. You may feel attacked because you have made things personal by allowing your emotions to react to whatever is undesired. This is the predictable response that corresponds with the large letter at the top of the eye test chart. In this scenario, a situation does not play out like your vision said it would, and the door of frustration opens itself to you. Allow these moments to be your eye test. The truth is that every day we are presented with things that will serve as an eye test if we allow them to and chose to see them in that light.

Some things that test the eye are of more obvious matters and are linked to addictions. Addiction works by crippling the ability to shift the mind because the lesser self (your form and senses) has literally become dependent on a substance or sensation that is either over-indulged in or unnatural to the body. This is like having one eye stronger than the other. This distorts our vision and causes us to see things only through our stronger eye. When someone has an addiction, their sight comes from their lesser lens only. Often times, our greater eye may realize that we want more for our life but cannot follow through or act in ways that will bring about better things. This is because its view has been obstructed or completely covered up. Environment is another element that strengthens the lesser eye by controlling what the eye sees in form. This could be a person that lives in a poverty stricken area. It could also be a child that grew up in the foster system having no consistency in who they see as a caring adult to serve them as a parent in their lives. These things strengthen the lesser eye in a way that makes it almost impossible to use the greater eye because things seem so blurry when you try to see things through the greater lens. Eventually, you will not bother trying to use that lens at all. Instead, you learn what you must in order to survive in the environment you are in.

This is the fish born into the aquarium. Maybe they have heard of a world full of possibilities and belonging. The harsh reality of their environment has not allowed them to see past what their surroundings tell them. Failure to pass the eye test results in a direct influence of what you see also becoming your reality. A person's environment pacifies them to become willing to accept more of what they see as their fate.

If a person has a vision issue, they must see an optometrist to provide the means to balance what is seen out of each eye. This gives each eye an equal opportunity to make sense of what is seen. In the same way, if you are battling addiction or environmental elements, you must neutralize what the lesser eye takes in by controlling what you allow your senses to come in contact with. Reducing the negative stimuli that makes the lesser stronger connects to all of the things that are related to what you take into your body through your mouth, eyes, ears, touch, and environment. All of these play into your senses and stimulate reactions from the lesser presence of who you are, causing you to see things from a very foggy lens. Remember, through this lens, no solution can be seen. But you are in control of the things that you allow to come into your body by what you take in through your mouth, eyes, ears, touch, and environment. This is what gives our greater lens an opportunity to feed the mind from its perspective, and equalizes the balance of what is seen through each eye.

Success and Failure

Success and failure seen through a healthy eye are one in the same, except failure is a catapult to future success. This leaves success as the barrier to further progress. Although we desire successful outcomes, they are more frequently the endpoint to our progress rather than the inspiration to new beginnings. Seeing the uniqueness in both failure and success allows us to not become overtaken by either of them. Instead, we can use failure for the information you will receive from it. We can use success as an indicator of our ability to persevere as we implement self-discipline to accomplish the things in life that we have set forth to do. Solutions are in both of these elements because failure is a byproduct of success. Once you have failed enough, a success formula is learned and can be repeated. Therefore, success is only constant acts of self-discipline after information has been received from failure. This is the case so that this success can be attained more than once.

Solutions cannot be seen unless your vision is clear. With a clear vision, the new battleground comes between you making the best choice out of others that are merely good and better choices. So in everything that you do, there is a good choice, a better choice, and the best choice. It takes continual mindshifts to monitor the thousands of moments that you make decisions throughout each day. To evaluate each decision that you make in a day and survey whether it is the good choice, better choice, or best choice takes your ultimate self in its fullest capacity. This matter is so relevant that the topic being evaluated could be as simple as what you choose to eat for breakfast. These small circumstances are what build up the quality of life. Unfortunately, "good" choices are not enough to make one as successful as we typically desire. It takes the best choice to become the person that you wish you were. Constant mindshifts are the only way to accomplish this as it is what maintains successful outcomes.

Everything that we do should be evaluated under this light, so we can use success and failure to guide us in the way it has been designed. If you experience failure, take the information it provides to map out three different responses: good, better, and best. Of those choices, select the best way to go about responding to that failed experience. When you experience success, you can use the same principle. Many times in my career as a player and coach, a game would be won but disappointment would follow the victory because the game was played "well" and not at the "best" level possible.

Good - Growing up, I lived exactly one mile away from my elementary school. So my siblings and I would walk home from school with the other neighborhood kids. One day as we were walking home, I noticed a beer bottle in the lawn we were passing, so I picked it up! Noticing that there was a little swig left in the bottom of it, I chose to finish it off. I remember it like it was yesterday. It was a glass bottle of Red Dog beer. The warm, backwashed beer was disgusting, and I immediately spit it out. I guess I had some ride-or-die friends because the pact that we made stood, and nobody told a sole. It turned out to be a pretty good choice because my parents never found out, but it opened the door to my curiosity to substances.

Better - Imagine six boys living in a four-bedroom house with one bathroom (not to mention my five sisters). That was the majority of my childhood. In the winter in Kansas, there is about four months that you can't play outside, so we played in our room. *Teenage Mutant Ninja Turtles* and Bruce Lee movies always inspired us to fight after watching them. One day, we had a ninja fight and my brother Larry was drop kicked in the chest as I flew from one bed to the other bed that he was standing on. His butt hit the sheet rock so hard that it created a hole in the wall. Panic struck us all, and we immediately put our heads together to develop a plan. We decided to hang a poster over the hole in the wall. This would prevent our dad from giving us all whoopings! Not a bad idea, huh? Well, it postponed the whoopings for about a month or so. Still worth it in my opinion. Who knew, the world could have ended before he found out! The fury following a "same day" whooping would have far exceeded the emotions a month or two out. I think we easily made the "better" choice.

Best - My sister Laryee got pregnant her senior year of high school and contemplated having an abortion so mom and dad would not find out. She was seventeen years old at the time. Our family's reputation was on the line as we were seen as perfect in the eyes of the community and church. Eleven respectful and well behaved kids, same mom and dad. We were highly respected as we stood out as one of a few black families in a predominately white suburb. She decided to have the baby. This shook the family. However, this event ended up drawing the family closer as my parents supported Laryee and never made her feel less than. Laryee went on to get her undergraduate degree from Rockhurst University in Kansas City, MO in economics, finance, and Spanish. She then went to the University of Kansas and earned her doctorate degree in International Business and Law. Her daughter Morgan is currently studying Behavioral Neuroscience at Boulder University.

It is safe to say that Laryee made the best decision that could have been made in this scenario.

Money

Finances are a topic that everyone can relate to because there are problems for every financial class. Everyone wants more money because it is portrayed as the thing that can fix our issues. As you gain a better understanding of the formless, world money rapidly loses its value because anything that is physical (including currency) is only seen as a reciprocal to one's ability to manipulate the formless world around them. Proper manipulation of the formless world requires money to come and find you. Unfortunately, a frequent stigma seems to be that people are going out and looking for ways to find more money. There is a demand for your gift, which is inside of your purpose. This gift was created in you and was given the same uniqueness as your actual fingerprint; this gift cannot be imitated or recreated. This will bring you the lifestyle that fits your purpose. If more money is in the formless plan for your life, it will show up but only if your formless purpose requires more of it.

For those of you who say, "More money is what I need, and it will fix all of my problems, or at least make life a heck of a lot easier to deal with," I respond in great confidence that the solution to your concern is rather simple. Attaining the physical things of the world can be accomplished merely based on work ethic. If you are willing to compromise your integrity, gaining income becomes an even easier task to accomplish. Those seeking money rely on a variety of things: work ethic, cunningness, job, level of education, the casino, the lottery, other factors leading to job security, and more. People such as these exist to pay off debt, own a car, own a house, and travel the world. It is important to notice that these things can be done without fulfilling your purpose, which is why none of those artifacts can keep a person happy on the inside. This person would be the fish that lives in the aquarium and be completely content with the limitations that comes along with it.

Just as the lottery distributes millions (or at times billions) the Formless Intelligence distributes hearing, sight, speaking ability, the functional ability of your body, and the rest of your senses. Would you trade your sight and hearing for one billion dollars? My guess is that you would not, which makes the values of astronomical amounts of money minuscule in comparison to the things that cannot be given to you by man. This is why when parents are asked about expecting a child, they always respond with the hope to have their child born healthy. And who do the parents place this hope in? The Formless Intelligence. Or if a rich man is on his deathbed and never believed in a higher power, before he dies, he says a prayer just in case and bargains his past good deeds along with his wealth for acceptance in the afterlife that may or may not be. Who is he praying to or bargaining with? The Formless Intelligence.

If you are taking in the principles presented to you in this book, you will value money less. Instead, you will regard your purpose, along with the non-measurables of this world, with a much greater respect than the respect money is often given. You will have placed your hope in the unknown, knowing that no matter how distinguished you are, you do not know very much at all even when you are compared to things that are known. You will know how the power of a mindshift works and use them to empower you to apply knowledge to you actions. You will believe that money is attracted by the development of the gift inside of you, which turns you chasing after money into you chasing after your purpose. Your purpose will earn your living and keep you at peace on the inside. Money will buy you something that will be old in six months, and in a year, the purchased thing that was once your pride will become your biggest annoyance.

Your purpose expressing itself through your form is priceless, and money that acts as compensation for you not living out your purpose will never be where your joy comes from. By now, you understand that your purpose is more valuable than any dollar amount that could be named.

CHAPTER 8
SUMMARY

In everything there is a good, better, and best choice. Evaluate all that you do so that you are making the better, or best choice throughout the many decisions that you make within a single day. These mini victories are what add up to creating the life you desire for yourself. Understand this:

- The solution is the exact opposite of what being the victim embodies.
- To understand solutions, you must realize the battle inside of you between the greater and lesser presence of who you are.
- Even when you find a solution, there was a better one out there, no matter what (Good/Better/Best).
- Solutions can be found through the lesser lens, but they are never desired in the long term.
- Solutions found in the greater lens are more beneficial, especially in the long term.
- You must train through constant mindshifts.
- Can you pass the eye test and operate by seeing with 20/20 vision?
- Money only reciprocates the value of a person's values.

PART 3

9

THE LAW YOU SHOULD KNOW

"What you see as light is what motivates you to attain what the light gives you access to see."

-LaDrew Murrell-

The law you should know can be explained in the contrast of light and dark, which will act as a medium for *knowledge and unawareness*. There is a light that radiates inside of you starting at your center and expanding outward, according to your level of consciousness. If the light inside of you is dim, you will experience many difficulties due to ignorance, which produces its equivalent in calamity. Without this light, you cannot persevere, and the darkness then multiplies itself within you, increasing the misfortune you experience by the simple means of being unlearned in that area. In this chapter, you will learn that what you do not know will lead to your demise, therefore ignorance is not bliss; it is deadly.

The law is like works like this:

Imagine a conveyer belt, like the one you would see on an assembly line in a factory. Only, imagine thousands of them many miles long, all leading to a large dark pit. On these belts are words written like: religion, denominations, war, politics, alcohol, drugs, tobacco, sex, adultery, gluttony, depression, anxiety, greed, perversion, money, envy, anger, fear, dishonesty, divorce, debt, hopeless, poverty, stress, insecurity, and misfit. On each belt, there are people lined up one after the other, for as far as the eye can see. There are so many people, the words on the belts had to be repeated many times over on multiple conveyor belts. The belt that each person stood on was the one that their greatest weakness lead them to. All the time, people left one belt only to arrive on another, eventually returning back to the belt they were on before. Randomly, some people were lifted off of the belt as though they climbed to a higher realm. The belts moved rather slowly, so slowly in fact, that you could stay on any conveyer belt for two decades before falling into the pit. Every second, thousands of people fell into the pit.

In the pit, people climbed onto one another trying to get out, while others seemed very content to be inside. It seems that the company of other people around them, especially friends and family, made the pit feel like a safe place. Many times, people escaped the pit and ran in the opposite direction that the belts rotated in, passing others on the left and the right. The people on the belts did not seem to notice them, but once they got tired of running, they would go onto the belt that aligned with their feelings. These people would end up back in the pit, and they would live there and raise families there, placing their children on the same belt that led them into the pit.

The belts were dark, so dark that they engulfed the feet of the people standing on them like quicksand. All the time, people would try to step off of the belt but it stuck to their feet like tar and would not loosen its grasp. This would make it difficult for the people to get off of the belt. The belt even had power to provoke each person with more of its identity to keep the people on it. The belt could do this because the people were ignorant of the means to confront the words written on the belt. In fact, they would just become more of the word written on the conveyor belt they stood on. Each belt was in competition with the other belts, wanting to be full of people to take to the pit. The more people each belt brought to the pit, the bigger it got. So rage competed with alcohol, and alcohol with tobacco, and tobacco with stress, to the last.

The pit was so big, it looked like there was room for twice as many people, but there was no natural light in the pit. Everything there was artificial and man-made. But there were very nice looking structures in the pit, and people could even grow vegetables under the lights made for the pit. There were streets and cars, and people held jobs there. But in the pit, each person was identified by the belt that led them there and lived near others that came into the pit by the same means. Their identity was on a badge, and it could get them into certain places, but not every place. The pit was evil because it pretended to be good. It kept the people comforted by their lack of understanding. The pit allowed every person to embody the victim mindset so it could use everyone's weakness as its means of success. Every person seemed so dark in the pit, and no light came from them. Light only came from the things that they possessed. In the nicer neighborhoods, the cars, homes, cell phones, and more materials like this held a lot of light and did not fade quickly. In the poorer places, anything that held light would not last long at all. This caused people in poverty to look for new light in anything that they could find.

From the pit and the belt, you could see people rise to a higher realm, which would shine light on those below. Sometimes, people would ascend because someone came to get them and other times because they used a mindshift to elevate themselves above the circumstances that was leading them into the pit. Although removed, they could always see the conveyor belt and pit, which would tempt them to go back. Sometimes they would go back but most times they would not.

The people above would shine their light on those below and provoke them to learn the ways of freedom through mindshifts, but the people of the pit and on the belts did not have control of their minds yet. They would act as mentors to those on the belt or in the pit, teaching them things that would give their mind power to shift. Many of the people above had the same possessions as the people below, except no light came from the possessions in this realm. Light only came from the people here. Everything that was built by the hands of man was extremely dark but these things became illuminated once someone possessed it.

This illustrates the law you should know. It is the contrast of how darkness and ignorance will impede your mind and the mind of your offspring until it ruins it all, so much that you cannot shift out of the realm of darkness. People experience life in light and darkness because no one can become wise in all areas of life, which is why, at some point in their lives, every person was on a conveyor belt. This is the power and guarantee of darkness; it has something to feed on inside of every person because no one has lived a perfect life, or is immune to temptation. So the memories of your past, and the temptations of the things that you should not engage in, will provoke you for an entire lifetime. All the while, others will live by a light that is artificial, sometimes knowingly but in most cases, the fact that light in the pit is artificial is unknown to those residing in the pit.

Darkness

What you do not know is a direct reflection of the problems that are present in your life. What you are driven by are the means to keeping you in ignorance as these things become your convictions. A person's convictions are so deeply grounded in the subconscious mind that constant, intentional mindshifts are the only way to remove them. These convictions will allow unhealthy habits to rule, even though you wish they would not. They will even have you substitute a lie for the truth for the sake of your argument. If you are unlearned in marriage, you will be challenged with the factors that lead to divorce and eventually become divorced. And if you are unlearned in finances, you will likely end up in debt or other undesired financial grips. If you are learned in finance, but not in self-disciplined, the darkness will misuse the finances by way of ignorance to your ability to apply self-discipline. Darkness will use itself to work its way into learned areas in your life, so you must always be aware of the dark areas within yourself. In this way, a person's ability to obtain money will not create a highway to acquiring the things money can get them that they are not self-disciplined enough to resist.

Many are motivated by things that do not hold the light of life in them, like houses, cars, luxury, money, status, and fame. In the pit, these things give light to those seeking them, and when they are attained, the light they provided dims and allows one of their counterparts to appeal its light to the same person so that they are always seeking new forms of darkness. And eventually, you prefer the darkness over the light. This person is not more fortunate than the infant child who passed away seemingly before their time.

How much more dreadful is it to live long in years only to have never lived by the true light of the world?

Darkness works like this: There was a man who lived in the pit. He came there by loneliness, insecurity, pornography, theft, deceit, alcohol, and tobacco. He had many things that gave him a sense of pride and shone as light to him and all of the people around him. His watch and car shined brighter than anyone else's, and he worked extremely hard to acquire them because they were his dream possessions. But, as time went on, the light held by these things began to dim and people stopped following him because he was losing light. He worked very hard to get new things with new light, and he did. People again came because they were attracted to the light until the day he became too tired to chase these lights. On this day, he became consumed by the darkness inside of him because there was not enough false light to distract him from it. On this day, he chose to take his own life. In the pit, the darkness used the same principles to subdue the rich man, the poor man, and the middle school child. Their identity and purpose were kept dormant inside of them.

No person can be fully illuminated in light because of their past memory of dark behaviors. This gives the darkness a chance to fulfill its goal in our life for as long as we live. The darkness inside of us recognizes what is also dark in others and latches onto their unawareness in order to grow their dark areas and ours. This creates barriers to the light inside of us. Areas that act in darkness in your life will always be connected to the areas that act as darkness in the lives of the people that you are closely connected to. This is because the darkness inside of someone else can pull you down in the same way as light can pull someone up from the darkness.

Darkness uses time against its prey because it is aware of the law of time. Since those living in the darkness are oblivious to the law of time, their time is given to more of what has them living in darkness. Again, take the man that is in the pit by way of loneliness, insecurity, pornography, theft, deceit, alcohol, and tobacco. The darkness inside of this person will have them grasp onto the loneliness felt in their life fill it with pornography in their free time. Through the law of time, this repeated cycle can only become an addiction in the future. The darkness becomes overwhelming because it has partnered itself with the time you spend. This also dictates how your money is spent. This means that the reason that you go to work to gain money for yourself is only to buy more of what you spend your time on, time owned by the darkness in your life.

Light

The law of light and knowledge has everything to do with what is being used to provide you with sight. Your greater self cannot see from artificial light; only your flesh can do that. Therefore, any light that is not acknowledged by your higher self is not light that should be used for guidance. False light will ultimately lead you into the pit because, sooner or later, it will become dim. What you see as light is what motivates you to attain what the light gives you access to see. In poverty, these things act as light: cash, nice cars, designer cloths, jewelry, diamonds, gold, a house in the hills and other things with a fancy appearance. In the upper class, these things act as light: costly possessions, convenience, financial power, status, and acknowledgement. To the greater self, light is seen through the following: God, love, grace, time, nature, ideas, and your mind because these things are of immeasurable value and cannot be taken away from anyone. What is formless is freely given to everyone without limit.

What you see as light motivates you and will be on your mind when you go to sleep and when you wake up. The poor man wants more cash, and the rich man wants status above his peers. Both will do whatever needs to be done to acquire these things because they are both ensnared by darkness. But the person governed by the greater-self sees light in these things: love, forgiveness, faith, servanthood, compassion, empathy, giving, perseverance, knowledge, health, wisdom, and understanding. These attributes will give that person what the rich and poor man are seeking. But this way, no light is found through the material obtained by the man who is of the light. The greater self does not seek these things and is not motivated by them, so the level in which they come does not change the source of light.

In the example, each conveyer belt acts as a source of light to the individual on it, although it is darkness. The label on it gives the person an identity and a light to see the world with. It makes you believe that it is the only source of light there is. If you are on one of these conveyor belts, it is likely that you are motivated by the label of the belt you are standing on. You would also see the world through the lens of the word on the belt that you identify with. Even if it is depression, that aspect of who you are will be at the front of your mind when you go to bed, when you wake up, and when the first opportunity presents itself, depression will latch on to something that it can become depressed about.

If you live in true light, you are not persuaded by artificial light, therefore you are unmoved by it when life's circumstances go up and down. A person that lives in the true light has a solid foundation because what that person's foundation is built upon cannot be taken away by life's circumstances or opinions of others. A person of light is a producer. This can be the case because what is on the inside of each person of light is what they work to reproduce. This product requires the following from the person of light: love, forgiveness, faith, servanthood, compassion, empathy, giving, perseverance, knowledge, health, wisdom, and understanding. Therefore, what is produced by this person can continuously be reproduced by them, costing them only formless abstracts to reproduce their product. In this way, the person of light becomes a resource to others with a product that cannot be imitated by anyone else. This is the driving force and purpose of their life. This fills every void that form of any kind cannot fill.

I consider myself a person living in the true light. I have my mind and complete control of my thoughts, which have allowed me to write this book, all from thinking by way of mindshifts. From the light that is radiant through me, I will teach my sons how to avoid divorce and that college is not the only means to become a learned individual. I will teach my sons how to escape the grasp of poverty in all aspects of life so that they may become rich in everything that cannot be measured. I will teach my sons how to maneuver through a world surrounded by debt so that they are not overcome by debt themselves. I will teach my sons that they must produce, and whatever they should produce was planted inside of them when they were conceived. It is our purpose to commit ourselves to finding our fingerprint so we can live as a whole being in this world.

We should live a life that shines light on others by way of the platform we stand on: parent, brother, sister, teacher, friend, neighbor, doctor, and the like. Or we allow the darkness within us to influence those we come in contact with, giving those people a sense of comfort that they will not be alone if they share the same darkness, or that it is hereditary and cannot be avoided. Either way, the light within you (even if it is dark) will shine on others. I will teach my sons the difference between "things" possessing light and being the light yourself. That light radiates inside of us and illuminates the "things" we possess, not the other way around.

This is our obligation: to become a person of light, to become a producer, and to bring others to the light starting with your friends, family, and loved ones.

Problems You Face

Look at all of the things you have faced in your life—even the things that are out of your control that you may contribute to genetics or the environment you were born into. These are the things that gain access to minimize us in our own eyes and distort our view so that we cannot see what is within ourselves. This lack of knowledge acts as a co-signature to your own self destruction. You may be familiar with a situation like this: A person is unhappy with their spouse, so they tell themselves, "I'll be better off out of this environment; I will be a happier person, resulting in being a more present parent. So yes, divorce is the best option," or "Everyone in my family is overweight. That is why I am overweight. Disease runs in my family, so I will also get this certain disease and be overweight." When ignorance cosigns itself, it places you in an even darker space. Staying married is only a result of first knowing yourself and then choosing the right spouse. If you are on the conveyor belt, or in the pit, this is not a time to choose a spouse because it will likely result in you selecting the wrong person as a mate. Most people get married in this scenario, and you now understand that the light in this relationship cannot last. The false light that the relationship was built upon will dim over time and eventually become dark. Blaming genetics is also darkness cosigning darkness, as we all have seen people defy the odds of mental sickness, deformity, and obesity to become their ultimate self, despite the family they were born into, or the limbs and senses they were born with defect. My youngest son, whom I am proud of, has overcome a physical birth deformity, a deformity that held me in darkness for many years, filling my understanding full of excuses of why he would not be able to excel in sports.

So the problems you face are there because you have either cosigned ignorance with ignorance or because you are oblivious that you are struggling in a specific area. Without self-discipline, you will not overcome the problems you face. You must elevate to a higher view, like the view from above where you can see solutions. Seeing your problems face to face may overwhelm you and inspire you to dive deeper into the dark.

If you are in debt, look at the things that got you into debt and how ignorance played its part in that. Your viewpoint substitutes itself for time. A higher viewing lens, like that of a press box on a football field allows you to make better choices in the moment. This saves you from wasting time. Just as you can now look back in time and choose a better path to minimize your debt, you can also govern your choices through your higher self to make these same choices in real time. In that vital moment where decisions are made, create a powerful mindshift to decisions that are closely related to where you actually want to be in the future.

Think about your insecurities and how much they are magnified in your own eyes when you look into the mirror. Think about your opinion of what people think about you or say about you and how this obstructs your view from seeing the inside of you. Even people that are physically fit and pleasant looking are still self-conscious; social media proves this. As long as your opinion of yourself is tied to your form, you will remain in the dark about your true beauty, the beauty that is inside of you. This problem you face will last a lifetime as you look into the mirror each day and see yourself only through what the mirror shows you.

The key to overcoming the problems you face is not taking them on face to face, but from the realm of your greater self versus your lesser self. Nothing lesser stands a chance against what is greater. You are greater than what you see!

Knowledge of the Law

Knowledge of the law implies that you use what is constant and predictable to lead you through the journey of life. The light is illuminated through things that have the Formless Intelligence as its source. This is the only consistent place information can be received in a world that is constantly changing due to the law of time. Understanding the difference between light and darkness is to live through a reflective lens with the understanding that everything in form changes according to its time. This knowledge is the foundation of the law you should know.

Examine the part of your life when you were unaware of this law and lived as if it did not apply to you. Since the universe knows these things, imagine how easy the conveyor belts that you occupied had it when it came to facilitating your life. You were in a fight without even knowing about the fight; thus, the competition between the belts turned into a collaborative means to ensure that you would end up in the pit. And an easy task it was. But the knowledge of the law makes the experience on the belt a much different experience for the belt and the person on it.

In the process of complete consciousness, a person starts to become illuminated from within. As truth becomes known, the knowledge of the law makes each conveyor belt become powerless because it operates only on false principles. What was once seen as tar grasping the sole of your shoes was only an illusion of your mind, and you recognize that you are able to move freely from space to space. The power of this knowledge is that it puts your life back into your control, removing the illusion of victimhood and replacing it with a lens that can see solutions. As the light that wants to become radiant within you begins to work within you, each belt that has lured you in now becomes fearful of your knowledge of the law because its chances of losing your occupancy has increased because your mind has become part of you. Due to your knowledge, the belts shrink in size and become so thin that they are uncomfortable to stand on.

Now think of the belts that once occupied your time and energy (or possibly are still a struggle for you) and how the light within you has kept you away from complete annihilation. Knowledge of the law uses the simple foundational implications of the law of time in the sense that all things of form must change and are changing. According to law, no matter where you are(on a conveyor belt, in the pit, ascending to a higher realm, or living in the light) time will run its course and change your current state. Knowledge of the law allows you to always be working toward what you know is better, and even when you have attained what is better, this understanding will have you work twice as hard to maintain it until it runs the course of your life. This understanding makes nothing a surprise and everything a possibility. Controlled mindshifts are the application of this law, and choosing the greater is conviction in the law. Therefore, knowledge of the law does not make you immune to the elemental forces of the world that reels you into the pit by way of the conveyor belt. Only subconscious conviction to what is greater can save you from self-destruction.

Studies suggest that many women are most fit in their adult lives at the time of their wedding. By applying exercise and a healthy diet, this can be accomplished as long as it is done with fidelity. Much money will also be spent on supplements and beauty products to ensure that their most beautiful self will be presented to their spouse on that day. Knowledge of the law states that only true conviction will keep the woman in her best physical state, otherwise her mind will become weakened and light once obtained will be lost. This is how a person under the law becomes lost and ends up back into the system that leads to the pit. The greater self was not convicted due to conviction from within. Instead, opinions of others and wanting to take great pictures were at the root of action. As the inspiration faded after the wedding, so did the conviction.

Use of the Knowledge of the Law

There are many people in the world right now living a life very similar to yours. Almost the exact same story with the same problems. So, what is the difference between people who inherited similar circumstances in life but one is destroyed by this condition, and the other is driven to greatness by this same misfortune? Use of the knowledge of the law.

Your problems work for you; just as a king/queen has servants working under them. Your problems are here to serve you so that you know the areas in your life that need a mindshift. This will provide course correction in a way that will elevate your view in the moment. Seeing your "problems" in this light will change your opinion towards the things you call hardship, or worse, the things that you call addiction. Let the law work for you so you can continue to elevate yourself because the law was made in a way that will always allow you to improve no matter how well you are doing, or how badly you are doing. It will show you errors in your best work, allowing you an opportunity to make it better, only if you are able to see the law at work in the work that you produce.

Use of the knowledge of the law means that you are constantly looking for the sign; the sign that is showing up that gives insight to the better way. For a person that is not on the conveyor belt, "the better way" or "the sign" is close to obvious; but to the person in the pit or in the realm of those of darkness, "the better way" or "the sign" is often overlooked or not seen at all. This is because although there is one good answer, there is always a better one. Make it your goal to choose the things closest to the best choice, because choosing the good choice is never good enough. This can only be done by a mindshift in the moment.

All form is changing, even right now as you read these words. It is in our best interest to have the form in our life to change for the better. How can the use of the law stop harmful acts from occurring in your life or in the life of your loved ones. It cannot because the law gives everyone free will without interrupting their choices. This means there will always be a chance that you or a loved one will be victim to the dark acts of another individual. But if you are the light that is illuminated in the lives of those you love, if they are on a conveyor belt or in the pit, they now have a way out. Use of the light inside of you minimizes the possibility of certain acts occurring in your life because it is not as likely that you will be in the wrong place at the wrong time. A person cannot divorce if they are not married, or a teen cannot have a child if they are abstinent. A person cannot become addicted to nicotine if they never use the product, and a person can never become an alcoholic if they never drink. Having no acquaintance with the memory or feelings of these sensations robs the darkness of its power due to the use of the knowledge of the law.

The law teaches us about how time and adolescence, which causes a natural lack of understanding, will allow the darkness to have its season just as the moon is guaranteed its time. This season is created by darkness, placing itself as a barrier to the light. In these times, it is critical for a young person to have the light of a parent, mentor, coach, teacher, pastor, or friend to pull them away from that darkness. Although the memory would have been created, the light cannot be overtaken by a dim darkness.

There is only one way to defeat the memory of bad experiences: to recognize them when they enter the mind and immediately mindshift out of that space. This is the only remedy because once a thought has been acted upon, it is impossible to forget. This is a heavy penalty for wrong doing. So then, the mastery of mindshifts are necessary for everyone. Otherwise, the poor choices along our journey have a place of residence in our minds, which allows a memory barrier to form between ourselves and progress towards our ultimate self.

There is a darkness inside of us all, but the use of this knowledge will change how we deal with the people in our lives, especially our spouse and children. Before the marriage, you are aware that trouble will come, so where will the light come from in that time of trouble? Before you have children, you know that they will rebel and worry you to the point of death, but where will the light come from in that time of trouble? Before you bought the puppy, you knew that it would make a mess in the house and need costly veterinarian care, but where will the light come from in that time of trouble? As a parent, spouse, or young adult, you know what is at your fingertips with the power of the internet, but where will the light come from that will prohibit the engagement with negative apps or sites? The light must come from the inside of you.

I'm sure that we can all remember a time when a parent did not allow us to go somewhere, do something, or hang out with a certain person. Sooner or later, something bad happened, and you were either at that place, doing that forbidden thing, with the wrong person, or you were not. The story is now part of your life, and this is the use of the law or lack thereof. Did darkness act as a barrier to light, or did light keep you from the clutches of darkness?

Use of knowledge is the antidote to darkness. Become an expert in how to get back up in life by your own light or from the light that someone in your life shines on you. Become an expert in helping others get up after they have fallen. Become an expert in preventing yourself and others from falling by recognizing true light when you see it from the inside of yourself and others. That is the use of the knowledge of the law you should know.

CHAPTER 9
SUMMARY

The cure to everyone's problem is knowledge, and the difference between knowledge and information is this: Knowledge is programmed into the formless self, making it the principle that you live your life based upon. Information is received and either disregarded or used for selfish gains. Everyone is programmed by something, and it is my goal through this work to make you aware of this statement so that you may become aware of your use of the law that we live under. I leave with you these two concepts:

- Light = Awareness or Knowledge
- Darkness = Unawareness or Cluelessness

To use this information through the problems that you face will take constant and controlled mindshifts. Do not neglect the fact that the problems you face are a direct result of what you are not competent in. This indicator of inefficiency is the source to your future progress. Use the knowledge of the law to aid you in the process of leading your life through the predictable factors of what is to come.

Everything in life is extremely predictable. It is in our best interest to be prepared for what is to come.

Allow your problems to work for you, and chose to see them in this light in order to maximize its ability to lead you to the answers that you have been searching for. These same problems are what provide the strength for your foundation so that you can build a structure on top of it that can outlast whatever storm that may come.

10

WORTHWHILE

"Without the freedom of the mind, source cannot be understood. This blinds the individual, causing them to latch onto form of the world as truth."

-LaDrew Murrell-

Buying More Time

This is a valuable concept that I would like to add before our journey ends. Although this has been alluded to throughout our conversation, I want to make sure you have a crystal clear understanding of what this means and how to accomplish it. Time is freely given and it does not discriminate one bit. Everyone gets the same amount of time each day. Although our time here on earth ends according to our own time, you can (and should) maximize your own time by buying more of it.

Without mastering the concepts in this book, buying more time is impossible. You must be aware of your every thought as monitoring your mind allows you to capture the moments that should be evaluated in the light. This enables you to create a mindshift that will allow you to recognize an opportunity for better effectiveness in the moment. Your instincts also play a large role in this process; if your instincts are not guided by the greater government within yourself, you will be prompted to make the wrong choice. You must be aware when darkness attempts to cosign ignorance. Once you are past this point, you can (and must) follow your instincts.

Buying more time is like this: Two men were digging for oil. Three years had gone by, and they dug deep without finding an oil cavity. The man that owned the equipment began to get frustrated at the time spent on the project without any benefit that could be seen. What he could see was the cost of keeping the operation running each day and paying hired staff. He saw his wealth wasting away with the potential of becoming a loss that would not be restored. The day came where he decided to call the operation off to search for oil in a different location. But his partner convinced him to continue to dig there. He explained that the three years of slow progress that was made in that location would be repeated in another location, so why not dedicate one more year to this spot. If oil was not found in that next year, pay for that years loss and relocate the project. The owner found value in his perspective and they continued to dig there. Nine months later, they hit the largest oil cavity found in the past two centuries.

If you view your life from the sideline perspective, you will often see giants that will discourage you from seeing solutions. Some of the things people face in life are far too big to face this way, just like the owner of the oil rig. But the counter partner bought more time by seeing from a solution view point and following his instincts. If they relocated, he knew that they would eventually find oil in that new area, but it may have taken another two to four years. By staying in the same location, they could have reached the same outcome in a shorter time if they did not start over. In this case, he bought more time by saving himself and his partner at least two years from digging in another location. With this time, new ideas were pursued and conquered.

You should look for opportunities everyday to buy more time. There are even minute opportunities that could gain you more time each day, which over time adds up to extra hours, days, weeks, months, and then years.

When you apply this skill, you will maximize your learned skill sets due to experience because you will examine each moment when you are presented with frustration, which is your key indicator that time can be purchased through that conflict. Now that you are empowered, you will figure out a more productive means in the moment instead of days, or weeks, later. You can come to that same conclusion in the moment and use those days and weeks to accomplish new goals.

Time is the most valuable thing you can purchase. It is so valuable that it cannot be purchased with currency; it must be purchased with the mind. Invisible stuff can only be manipulated by the part of you that is invisible. Connection to the Formless Intelligence gives you the ability to work with the formless world. The invisible time is always ticking but its values changes from person to person, and it is all dependent on whether their mindshifts are done consciously or unconsciously because this dictates how and where time is spent. Time spent working for a certain hourly pay or salary is worth that exact amount, however, time spent on thinking, reading, having conscious conversation, or doing is greater than the value of monetary things.

The concept of buying time may seem ordinary or obvious but to actually accomplish this takes a tremendous amount of self-discipline and conscious mindshifts. When you are proficient in buying more time, you will notice that your days seem long enough, and your tasks to complete are all capable of meeting their deadlines. Minds shifts in the moment and eliminating non-progressive activities add value to a person's time because conscious time adds value in form to that same person's life.

Live or Die

What does it mean to live, and what does it mean to die? No matter where you are in life, your reading up to this point can only allow you to see through the light inside of you. Living is connected to the law because you can only live life through the Formless Intelligence and its consciousness. To live apart from this consciousness is to live a life in the absence of your source. As a result, truly living is not a possible option. Think of someone who has made a great contribution to the human race positively. This cannot be done outside of a conscious state of something greater than themselves. Life is much more than acts to satisfy the body until tomorrow comes and the same feeling must be pursued again. Life itself is generated through the light inside of you, and outside of this light, one cannot truly live. Living is being present in the moment through mindshifts that allow you to reflect on your experiences in real time. When a person watches a movie, their attention is captivated in a way that allows them to stay focused on what they are seeing without having their mind drift off. Living in the light of the Formless Intelligence allows you to experience life through the formless contact that life interacts through without being intercepted by the desires of your flesh. To accomplish this, you must live in your purpose and be in complete control of your mind. This means no one is doing your thinking for you. Instead, you use every second of everyday to evaluate things that are happening around you and inside of you, so that the formless self is being developed.

    Let's look at the grass that we all appreciate. It is special because we know its purpose and, through obedience, it fulfills its purpose continually. In this way, it lives, provides life and continues to live on. However, you are only living if you are living out your purpose and in obedience. This creates relevance in your life in a way that will not allow you to be forgotten when you leave this planet. Thus, what you have contributed will be carried on through the inspiration you have given others by way of your platform. A person not living out their purpose everyday or working towards it is only sleepwalking; they are not living. They are dead among the living, because society dictates their thought patterns, and their environment is seen in unchanging respect. This causes the subject to chase their own tail in hopes to receive a reward. This person does not understand that what is being pursued is of no benefit; it only keeps you occupied by predictable methods. The more obvious cases are those that live life in an unaware state, such as those that are taken over by extreme mental illness or extreme drug abuse; these are easier cases to see those that are walking while sleeping, as a zombie like-state has overtaken them. But those that get up, go to work, keep a clean credit score, and play golf with their friends are much more difficult to identify because it is possible to have what is perceived as success and not experience life at all. You do not have to be buried into the ground in order to be dead. Neglecting one's purpose is to live under the influence of death.

 Darkness overshadows the light to those who are under its influence. This is how a person sleepwalking may think they are doing quite will. This is the person in the pit with so many things that the light that is provided by the things are worshiped like gods. These things keeps the person content with chasing after more stuff. But walking in life by living out one's purpose is like my mother Opal; although she did not have much, she had everything! Her life is full and her light is bright. Her light is seen by everyone that she meets, and I have witnessed people rich in the form of the world envy her because of the peace, joy, and love that she displays and has in her life. Yes, I have seen a person that has it "all" envy someone who has nothing in form at all. In her case, not having much in form but living in light gave her everything in abundance, with no debt or interest. It seems that no matter how much false light a person attains (cars, planes, boats, homes) it can never give them what my mother has so much of, and the monetary value of those possessions cannot come close to the value of the formless virtues she has.

You have the tools to truly live, and regardless of what you have in form, your purpose and the value of the light of life will far succeed the value of any possession that you once held in high esteem. This light has the authority to place formless elements in your light that cannot be obtained with money or given to you by a close companion. Never will a formless void be filled and made complete inside of you with the form of the world. When you live in your purpose, it fills the void in our lives that nothing else can fill. No matter how much money our fingerprint makes for us, the quality of life we live is enough because our void is filled with our purpose and fingerprint. This void is a void that no form can fill. This is a void that your fingerprint cannot fill unless your fingerprint is attached to your purpose.

Vision

We will end our journey of discovery in a new way of thinking with the most important law that you will need to understand because it impacts how you interact with the world and apply all of what is known by you, including what is known about the unknown.

Your vision determines what is appealing to you because vision holds onto your purpose. It is the gate to things becoming known by you and the foundation that is built upon for your purpose. Depending on what you believe about yourself and your purpose, certain acts will follow. With a clear vision and conviction in your purpose, all of the questions asked in the introduction can be understood and answered.

- Who am I?
- You are a formless being that is connected to the Formless Intelligence.
- What is my purpose?
- To be in complete control of your mind so that what is inside of you can become known.
- What is Truth?
- Truth in form is relative. Truth that is unchanging remains formless.
- How can I reach my dreams?

- By understanding the concept of source and properly using your time so that your purpose can become known by you.
- How can I know the unknown?
- Simply by knowing that it is more than your ability to understand and comprehend. The unseen, which is unknown, holds more weight than all that has ever been seen before.

With a clear vision, you are not easily distracted by things that do not align with your vision. What you see as an obstacle can be avoided when purpose is behind the wheel. As you are living out your purpose in chase of your destiny, your priorities towards it become a very strong bond, creating a barrier between who you are and things unlike you. If you can see clearly, who you are inside and what it is you are to do, it is very unlikely that simple things will throw you off course in your pursuit of the ultimate self. When you know who you are, loving yourself becomes natural because self-acceptance only happens through knowing your identity. Your identity is linked to your purpose, and it is your purpose that can be clearly seen that will keep you on the path towards it.

A person with vision can see who they are. When your identity is not hidden from you inside of the form of this world, you are able to know who you are not, and stick only to who you are. Identity is understanding accompanied by self-love, a love that cannot be received from anyone else. Vision allows a person to live a lifestyle of self-discipline. This person continuously does things that are associated with their purpose and identity. When you identify with the formless self and find your purpose through your identity, you are unwilling to compromise who you are for anything.

Where there is theft, murder, drunkenness, suicide, anxiety, depression, low self-esteem, drug abuse, use of tobacco, violence, gang activity, and the like, there is no vision. Identity plus purpose creates a vision that does not stumble over simple destructive behaviors listed above because nothing of form is recognized by vision as truth. Vision allows you to see the truth in the unseen and latch onto to the formlessness of the world with all of your hope.

Vision is what makes self-discipline easy. The New Year's resolutions do not last long because they do not align with that person's identity or purpose. This gives the resolution no chance in overpowering the will of the flesh when opposition to the goal set is presented. With the flesh, having easy access to fulfill its desires your vision must be extremely clear so that you are able to maneuver around what is not beneficial to you.

In education, there is a large focus on suicide prevention because the number one threat in a young person's life is themselves. Who can save a person from themselves? Blinded vision is the key element to ensnare the mind to create this catastrophe. Without the control of the mind, a person's purpose cannot be known. Without the freedom of the mind, source cannot be understood. This blinds the individual, causing them to latch onto form of the world as truth. This forces them to try to see what is ever changing as something that will never change. Without the ability to become whole, an imbalance sets in, which makes taking your own life an act to consider. To be blind is not to be without sight it is to see what is seen as unchanging truth.

My intent is to open your eyes and for you to inspire someone else to open theirs. The world that we all want to live in starts with our vision. We must see past what can be seen, looking past someone's shape, color, size, hair, religion, house, fame, or title. Instead, we must see them as a whole person: soul, mind, and body. We must recognize through their behavior, noticing if their vision is clouded, completely in need of restoring, or just fine. Then, without judging, we must help them through providing service and sharing love. In my tenure of teaching, I have always gotten along with all students, especially those that were labeled as "bad" because I know that there is no such thing as "bad" just "temporarily blind" due to circumstances in life. Showing someone who they are is tough business, but it eliminates an array of problems: teen pregnancy, drug abuse or experimentation, depression, self-hate, and the like. So these things are only indicators that a person's vision has been obstructed in a way that sees disruptive behavior as solutions to problems. If you make a persons vision clear, their behavior will change automatically, making the problem vision-related and not behavioral.

In any person with clear vision, you will notice an abundance of positive traits: self-confidence, self-discipline, self-love, intrinsic motivation, healthy habits, clean diet, clean speech, pride, humility, connection to Source, and the like. These people are a light to the blind which is what this world needs from you. In the pit, those that are there need light and latch on to form, which serves as an artificial light source. But, even a person who is blind in this sense can see your light through all of the qualities that make you different from most people. This will open their ears to hear you because their attraction to your light opens the gateway to them possibly attaining light themselves. This is how a person can be saved from the pit that has swallowed up many people by preying on the weakness of the flesh. All everyone wants is light, so they either seek light through acquiring things or through the formless things of this world.

I had a former athlete reach out to me on social media once. I didn't know why he reached out, but I responded immediately. I learned that he struggled with drug abuse, depression, and even contemplated suicide. But in their lowest time, they remembered me and felt that I truly cared for them. They remembered something that I told them and held onto it. It kept them from taking their life. What they held onto from the things that I told them was the formless things, about their life purpose and my belief in them. If I would have only praised him about the things he did in form: great blocker, tackler, intimidating physicality, and size, those compliments would have faded as his size, his physicality, and football-playing ability diminished due to drug abuse. But those few formless words held their value until his time of need, keeping their light and never fading, not even a little. All the while, the light from the accolades received from playing ball became as dark as the darkest night.

His vision was stripped away from him by his dependence on drugs and his struggle with identity and purpose. This equation gives life no meaning because without vision, purpose (which is your driving force) cannot be found. Any life without meaning will be lived loosely with no consistency, character, or structure to keep life on a track towards prosperity. So as we fight a suicide epidemic and all time highs dealing with depression, inclusion, and anxiety, combat these measures with formless abstracts that shine as true light, brighter than any artificial light that can be seen.

The Law of Truth

We should not leave without total awareness of what Truth is. We have learned from chapter one that the source of a thing is where the truth can be found. With this understanding, we can navigate around the barrier that our individual knowledge and understanding of truth provides us. Truth seen in light shows its law which is as constant as gravity is in its law. So truth is formless, unchanging, and expresses itself through your knowledge of its principals.

The law of gravity is well known, explored, and in our confidence of our understanding we teach it in schools. We have manipulated the principles of this law to enable us to defy the laws of gravity through our use of wingsuits, parachutes, aircraft machines, hot air balloons, and toys that fly in the air. Nevertheless, gravity has stayed consistent, providing us with an unchanging character to work with. In this way, no ones opinion of gravity changes what it really is; it is of the greater creation and will never be reliant on someone's defense, understanding, knowledge, belief, or action. Gravity is exactly what it will be, no matter what.

Truth is also like this: subject to the will and understanding of mankind, but not dependent upon human knowledge of its law. So truth can be denied, distorted, manipulated, defied, or slandered. But it never changes, no matter what we decide to do with it. So if gravity will allow one to explore their limits compared to their understanding, will it coexist with their theory or kill them to protect its character? In the same way, you can explore truth in any way you choose, but you will die before you are allowed to mismanage your understanding of the principle it was founded upon. Therefore, ignorance is not bliss—it is deadly.

Is there a such thing as something being true? Is there a God? Are there multiple paths leading to one truth? Can I make truth conform to what I believe? You can fill in the blank here with any question you may hold, but ask yourself this question: Can humans fly? Your answer to this is equivalent to the answer to all of your questions in regards to Truth. The Formless Intelligence has made all things this way: subject to the will, thoughts, and understanding of mankind, but not dependent upon these simple human elements.

I am sure that most of you reading this have flown on a plane, and on your flight, I am certain that you placed your confidence in that aircraft to fly you from one place to the other safely. But, was your confidence in the aircraft or the fact that gravity will never change its law, which will allow mankind to build a machine to fly through the air because of its loyalty and obedience to the Formless Intelligence? I am also sure that everyone reading this book has questioned if there is a God, and if there is, why has the world gone astray? But, do you also depend on the law of Truth when you hope to have a healthy child, seek health for an ill loved one, seek safety for a child that is sent to school, or hope that the difficult circumstances of life will one day come to an end? The truth will also remain obedient to its principle and the laws established by the Formless Intelligence so that we can be assured that what it is, it will always be.

There was once a man who lived in a small town. He had no wife or children, and no one knew his name. His days were spent taking walks, managing his garden, and reading on his front porch. He never spoke to people but would wave and smile to those who acknowledged him. In fact, he had only been seen talking to toddlers if their ball or toy had rolled to his feet as he sat on the bench in the park. No one knows what he said to them, and the children could not repeat it because they were not of talking age. But they would always run away leaping and smiling from ear to ear.

It was said that he lived off of the inheritance of his father. Misunderstood he was, and to make matters worse, he was not received well because his appearance was not seen as handsome. His skin was the color of charcoal after it has been consumed by fire. Everyone in that town mistreated him for reasons unknown. He was lied on, beaten, accused, framed, robbed, threatened, and not respected. He was tried on many occasions but never said a word in his defense, so he was thrown into prison and released time and time again. Even the guards of the jail mistreated him, spitting on him and beating him with their clubs. But still, not a word from the man. Because he was seen as poor and held no influence in the community, no one came to his defense.

One day in his old age, he shouted from his porch, "Today I will speak," and soon enough the word got out around town, and people came running to his front lawn to hear what he would say. After half an hour had passed, there stood every person in the town that could stand on their own two feet right in front of him; even the local news reporters came to his front door to broadcast the event for the elderly, ill, hospitalized, and incarcerated.

The old man said, "My name is Truth, and I am a reflection of your understanding. I have left for you a part in the inheritance left to me from my father." After he said this, he sat down and took a deep breath, closed his eyes, and passed away. And from his will the entire town was rebuilt beautifully.

CHAPTER 10
SUMMARY

Buying more time is essential to your future success as you are now using mindshifts to impact your life. To explain the simplicity of this teaching, I will offer how I purchase the majority of shares of my time. During the time that this book was written, I did not watch television. I replaced that time with mind growth activities as well as writing. I saw the benefits of buying time and the leverage I was gaining was in becoming valuable, and I began to buy more. I then gave up social media apps and only used them to share love for others and promote this project. I also stopped "going out" to places that did not promote wellbeing and did not align with the vision that I had for myself. This naturally separated me from many old friends and acquaintances, giving me even more time to mature in my gift.

To live is to produce a life that relies on predictability so that we can choose life over death. To live is to simply fulfill your life's purpose by submitting to the greater system of all things governed by the Formless Intelligence. To live apart from this system is existing without living a life in awareness and light. It is essential here to allow yourself the option of making this choice one that you make consciously. The choice here is between life and death. Choose life!

It could be said here that a person's vision is the most important aspect of their life. It is the essence that keeps their life on track and deems certain things as fitting or unacceptable. Our vision is what gives us insight not to compromise when temptation comes in the form of your past weaknesses. By all means, your vision must remain clear so that it is possible for you to stay the course.

I have also left you with the keys to buying time and Truth. With this, you should be able to do:

- Evaluate whether you are making the good, better, or best choice in the moment.
- Understand the cruciality of time and its effect on your life.
- Understand that Truth is so vast, it can be understood differently by every living person without changing itself.
- Know that we will all pass away due to our inability to act according to the principle of Truth with fidelity.

11

A KINGDOM, NOT RELIGION

"And I confer on you a kingdom, just as my father conferred one on me,"

-Luke 22:29-

Truth Seen Through Gravity

In an attempt to inform you of the truth, I would like to provide one last analogy for you to act as a medium for your understanding. Gravity is a concept that we understand (more so than Truth) very well as humans, however, they are both exactly the same as it relates to their source and principals. They are both very real and will protect their character, even if it means that you lose your life. Uncompromised integrity. Explore this explanation.

Like gravity, truth can be understood differently

by every living person at the exact same time. The greatness of these two elements are that vast. However, neither of them change, have changed, or will change. Truth further explained works in this way:

We are all familiar with the law of gravity because at some point in our lives we have been victim of its principle due to our misjudgment and understanding of the law of gravity. As we grow and mature, exploring and traveling become of interest, but how we choose to get to our destination differs: some people prefer to walk, others prefer to drive, trains are very popular, buses are common, some fly in planes or air balloons, helicopters, some people hike, while others ski, some skydive, and others use wingsuits to fly. No matter the method, gravity stays exactly the same, never compromising its integrity as it shows no favoritism.

Having the courage to wingsuit fly has everything to do with one's faith in the equipment along with their understanding of the law of gravity. Courage is required as anything great in principal will cause us to second guess things. Ask yourself this question: Would I jump out of a helicopter hovering over a mountain and use a wingsuit to fly down to land? If your answer is no (like mine) I don't blame you! Usually, we choose what we are comfortable with instead of challenging ourselves to grow and move outside of our comfort zone. Wingsuit flying requires you to grow in knowledge of the law of gravity and have faith that gravity will not change in principle while you are in mid-flight. It requires you to have faith and courage to the point that you would risk your life to experience the fullness of gravity.

Religion or Truth

Typically people select a religion that they are comfortable and obviously agree with. Even if your religion is to believe in nothing, that still falls under a belief system. The issue with this is that all of us are required to find truth on earth. To expect to find it in a religion would be very difficult since truth can afford to be misunderstood by all simultaneously. This means that every religion that is followed today likely has many elements that are wrong according to Truth.

There is nothing wrong with selecting a religion to follow. I personally feel that Christianity has gotten closer to Truth than the others. However, there are many denominations within Christianity, which is proof of the barrier between understanding and truth. Just like gravity, people select their means of travel. Some are scared to fly, so they travel by train. Others are afraid to wingsuit fly, but they will skydive. Likewise, people like to do as they please and ask for forgiveness each week to cleanse their conscious. So they may join a religion that allows them to confess their sins and be free as often as they'd like. While some believe that if you are baptized, you are free and clear to live as you please because you have taken the necessary step to earn eternal life. Choosing what works for you is not how truth works. It takes no courage to live this way.

Would you choose religion over truth? Although we can never completely understand truth, we must grow in knowledge of it daily and have courage as we pursue it in its fullness. We must get to wingsuit flying level in our understanding of truth. This means we must get out of our comfort zone, and challenge ourselves. We must believe in truth to the point that we would risk our lives for it, knowing that we are one mistake away from a fatal ending and that we are capable of using courage and faith combined to glide to a safe landing. If we do not get to a wingsuit level of understanding of truth, we have failed. Your choice in religion does not likely challenge you enough.

When you understand truth, you would die for it. You would forgive those who persecute you as they are doing it. You would forgive those who wronged you in the middle of the wrongdoing. You would have empathy on those who have harmed you and work towards a peaceful solution. You would give your life for the sake of others, in hopes that truth would be found through your own actions. Consider Dr. Martin Luther King Jr. and how he stood for truth and died for it, remaining nonviolent as he led a people to do the same in the midst of abuse. Without understanding the truth, taking such a stance would be impossible. Or again, consider Stephan, one of seven men chosen to evenly distribute food in the community in the book of Acts. He was said to be full of faith and the Holy Spirit (truth). His understanding of truth was challenged, and he was killed as a result. In his last words, he spoke, "Lord do not hold this against them."

This is a wingsuit-flying level of understanding of the truth. What else could make a person say this as they are being stoned to death, or what could make MLK not respond with violence? We must get to this level of understanding. The consequence of not doing so would mean possibly believing in nothing or adopting a religion instead. Notice that understanding truth never requires taking one's life. Instead, you would give your own. This is a difficult thing to accept.

A wingsuit professional still drives a car or flies on a plane. So there is nothing wrong with being involved with a church that spreads the gospel. Your charge is to be the representation of truth wherever you go. So I ask you, would you be willing to pursue the fullness of truth to the point that you would sacrifice your own life to understand it completely? Again, this sacrifice cannot include harming another person, but giving up your own life.

If you take what I am saying as truth, then this is a matter of a kingdom and not a religion. Truth is a component of the kingdom of God. Without understanding it, you cannot enter into it. This is why it is said that only few find the narrow path that leads to life.

Kingdom

Every kingdom has the following components (kingdomcitizens.org):
1. A King and Lord
2. A territory
3. A constitution
4. A citizenry
5. A law
6. privileges
7. An army
8. A commonwealth
9. A social culture

One day in the kingdom of God, two of his principles conversed in the headquarters of the law. Gravity and Truth enjoyed one another's company, especially over a game of cards. One day as they were playing, a new messenger full of distress and worry kept interrupting their game with disturbing news, after he had seen the people in the kingdom misusing the principles that were established by each of them. The messenger would run into the room of law and say to Gravity, "People are saying that they can fly. They are wearing suits with wings and jumping out of planes, and others are saying this because they are going from one end of the earth to the other in a day's time!" Unbothered, Gravity kept his gaze on his cards and replied, "I am what I am." A few minutes passed, and the messenger came frantically running back into the room of law to report to Truth what he has seen from the people. "New religions are being formed, and each believer thinks theirs is correct. They are even killing each other because of their views. Aren't you going to do something about this?" Unbothered, Truth kept his gaze on his cards and replied, "I am what I am."

An hour passed, but the messenger had seen something worse and ran to report his findings to Gravity. "Gravity, the people are doing many things to their bodies to prolong the days of their youth. They are pulling up areas of their bodies that you have made come down. Aren't you going to do something about this?" Again, Gravity focused on the game and replied, "I am what I am." A few minutes passed, and the messenger came frantically running back into the room of law to report to Truth yet again. "Truth, no one respects you, and most say that you are not real. People are making up their own truths and doing whatever they want. I heard someone say that everyone has their own truth and that people should believe whatever feels right to them. They are saying that abortion is okay and that if you feel like you are something different than your body says, chop it off and be the opposite. Surely, you are going to do something? Something must be done!" Truth replied without a blink, "I am what I am."

With his face downcast, the messenger began to walk out the door. But before he could open it, Truth spoke and said, "Tell them this. Anything they have said or done can be overlooked and left behind in the past. However, if they do not believe in me, they will never find me." With great hope, the messenger left to spread the word.

CHAPTER 11
SUMMARY

The sole objective of this chapter is to aid in the understanding that this is not a matter of religion. Religion has too many rules and regulations to keep up with, and I myself am not estitute enough hold such a difficult task. However, I can come under the influence and protection of the kingdom of God and Jesus Christ so that the requirements are to love the Father with all of my heart and to love my neighbor as I love myself. This ensures my citizenship based upon who I am and not a list of things that I must do.

In a kingdom, you act upon things because of who you are dependent on versus doing things in religious organizations to "get" a certain thing in return. In turn, what I do is because of who I am; there is no motive needed. Although I am inferior, my King and the kingdom that I am under is superior to all things on earth. This gives me authority to dominate the circumstances of this life because I serve a king that has conquered sin and death.

In my final attempt to bring understanding to Truth, if you are willing to accept this, I offer the foundation of Truth. This will allow you to explore it for the remainder of your life with the understanding that you will never understand it fully. However, if you fall back on this passage when your intellect cannot make sense of truth's greatness, remember this: as it is said in John 14:6, "I am the way, the **truth** and the life."

Kingdom > Religion

12

KING OF KINGS

"The unknown aspect of a thing or situation increases the qualification it has to earn your belief and faith in God."

-LaDrew Murrell-

Invisible

Everything that you want in life is actually invisible. Culture has sold us the opposing formula to govern our life: a see-it-to-believe-it mentality. The proper understanding would be to believe it because you cannot see it. Yes, that is correct. The unknown aspect of a thing or situation increases the qualification it has to earn your belief and faith in God. There are many things that won't be understood by you, and each and everyone of them will require you to have faith, hope, and belief that God will take care of all of your unknowns. Evidence of His investment in your life can be seen in the selfless act of wrapping the fullness of Himself in flesh like you and I.

Think of the thing you see that you want so badly and inspires you to work harder, study longer, and sleep less. Whatever that thing is, you are actually pursuing the invisible quality that becomes form in that exact same way. Everything in the world that matters most is still invisible because once things become visible and known by us, they lose value and soon become just another thing that was discovered, driven, or experienced. This entire book was created to allow you to understand the concept of the word God and how His invisible kingdom is what is to be pursued on earth. I have referenced God as the Formless Intelligence because that is a less confrontational way of referring to a power that has been misunderstood and misrepresented throughout history in a way that has created a powerful barrier between some and The Father, Son, and Holy Spirit. Even though doubt may still enter the mind, you have been given the authority to govern your own mind to explore the Truth in the Holy Scripture for yourself.

Without barriers, you can find out who you are. The things that you have, or don't have, will no longer compromise your soul by placing those objects in front of your relationship with God. The knowledge in this book is critical because it leaves you without excuse. You now know that what is greater (God) does not need the lesser in order to reign and rule over the earth. Your belief in Him will not change this truth. For non-believers, this content forces the heart to be opened in a way that will challenge any understanding presented to the mind. This work allows you to come to a sense of reason before catastrophe strikes you or a loved one in a way that backs you into a corner. When you can no longer depend on human medicine, when science cannot fix who you are not ready to lose, the invisible is called upon. Now you have an opportunity to connect with the invisible, living God before you are forced into a situation that gives you no other choice.

Maybe you have never been taught about God. This book has opened invisible pathways for your understanding. Now all you have to do is read the word for yourself, and it will speak to you through its text. Through the living word, your formless self will begin to awaken. Feeding this light will become your priority as it seeks to become radiant throughout your entire body. Accepting Jesus Christ as your Lord and savior is the first step in this process. This provides a formless covering over your life that will allow you to learn the truth for yourself without having to fear death or be choked by the sin that leads to death.

How to know this is the correct path? Reading this book validates that, but if that is not enough evidence, this is the only answer to sin and death. All other religions have no cure. It is the only kingdom that carries on with or without your belief in it. Believe it or not, your life is governed by it, and your afterlife is dependent on your connection to it while you are here. God's image has been polluted by man to man, with religion being the barrier. God created sex, and it is a good thing, but when the evil desires of the flesh comes and corrupts sex, it can become a bad thing. One of my loved ones has been subject to rape, so I am well aware of the evil sexual desires within humanity and the bad twist that can overtake a good thing. In the same way, Christianity has been polluted by the evil schemes and slandered to lead you astray. Man can corrupt anything, even what is good, but what remains formless cannot be destroyed or corrupted by man. Man can only destroy himself by his own actions due to lack of understanding formless principles. None of God's power has been lost. This Truth impacts the world and those who do not govern themselves according to this higher order. This is why you could be anywhere and experience an act of terror: school, church, sporting event, concert, home, political conference, or any other place that could be named.

    Not following God's desire for yourself looks similar all around the world. It is like this: A person is frustrated because of the difficulties that they experience in life, so they grow to depend on what can be understood by them and seen as reliable. So they trust in themselves and everything else that can physically be seen or manipulated. They question everything in the unseen world. They disregard its relevance because their inability to interact with the formless frustrates them, so denial of its existence, along with victimization, provides them with comfort. They experience many hardships in life, all of which they curse God for and question why a god would allow a world to run in such a destructive way, having no regard for even an innocent child's life. These same hardships often result in a staggering blow; if not financially, the turbulence is draining physically and emotionally. They have heard of Jesus, and they still place a small amount of hope in God because they know that there are many things that remind them that they are not in control: having a healthy child, waking up in the morning, being kept safe from acts of terror, or being cured from a terminal disease. However, this person would rather flow with the waves of the world, finding the company of many others in the same boat as a sign of safety. They live a life coping in ways that numb the physical mind and body. They remain in the dark.

Living in the light of Christ Jesus looks like this: A person goes through the same circumstances as the one described above. In fact, there are many others that have gone through (and are going through) the same trials. The difference is, in the light of Christ, you do not find it difficult to keep moving forward due to the fact that you have clear vision. Therefore the same exact experiences and hardships do not crumble this person because of their faith and understanding of the infallible word of God. This is the only difference, and in this way, they remain in control of their mind through the toughest of times, giving them peace and health. Using what is predictable to serve its purpose. What is predictable? Both positives and negatives things will come, have come, and are present.

Following Christ Jesus is the only guaranteed conviction that is beneficial to all because his ways and teachings cannot harm another individual or yourself. Through deep conviction and following the word, you will benefit yourself and others around you. Any violence that has been done on behalf of Christ is not supported biblically, so that argument is invalid. A better argument would be that it is too loving and forgiving of others and their wrong doings.

I could have just written a book to give you the formula to gain wealth in form as many self-help authors have done, but I would rather see your soul prosper. Now you have both the means to financial freedom and spiritual understanding. From the wealth that I have received in life, I only saw that it was fitting for me to also pass it along to you.

No longer can your own understanding of God get in your way of finding Him for yourself. You understand invisible principles, and with that understanding comes truth. Seeing something in form only confuses the mind because the eye cannot see the root or source of what is seen. This is because what is seen in form is only the physical appearance of a formless thought, a thought that is still developing and working towards an even greater progression. You are now empowered to see the inside of what you are looking at, including yourself.

Taking Ownership

Although what makes up who you are is invisible, who you have chosen to be is visible. It is important to take ownership in the choice that you have made to follow your flesh, or to follow the living God. You must be honest with yourself because you can only betray yourself if you are not honest with yourself when identifying your allegiance. This is stated in **Galatians 6:3,** *"If anyone thinks they are something when they are not, they deceive themselves (NIV)."* It is better to admit and consciously choose who you want to be, therefore, if a change is desired in your life, you will have a basis for what needs to be changed.

If you choose to depend on yourself as your source, follow your sensual desires, and seek out of life things that can be purchased with money, then you are better off recognizing the independence that you are declaring from God. Otherwise, He may never display grace in order for you to come back to him. **Romans 1:28** states, *"Furthermore, just as they did not think it worthwhile to retain the knowledge of God, so God gave them over to a depraved mind, so that they do what ought not to be done (NIV)."*

However, if you recognize God as your source, you do not have to live by form in a world driven by what is formless. **Genesis 1:26** states, *"Then God said, "Let us make mankind in our image, in our likeness, so that they may rule over the fish in the sea and the birds in the sky, over the livestock and all the wild animals, and over all the creatures that move* *along the ground (NIV)."* You will receive a lot of criticism for following Christ (it has always been this way) but take ownership that you chose this path. Also take ownership in the fact that often the best answer is, "I do not know" or no answer at all. We understand that humans spend their entire lifetime trying to become proficient in one or two areas and can't even manage that, so how much more unlikely is it that someone would learn everything about the word of God or, even better, God Himself.

You are either one that knows the Truth and seeks to further understand the Truth, or you are unlearned about the truth and desire that it does not become known by you. Fortunately, we are protected by this law found in **Matthew 7:18:** *"A good tree cannot bear bad fruit, and a bad tree cannot bear good fruit (NIV)."* No matter what is said by any person, their actions confirm what is in their heart, mind, and subconscious mind. You cannot take someone else's word for truth. In order for conviction to occur, you must learn what truth means for yourself.

So then, if you are a greedy person say, "I choose to be greedy with my time and money. I choose to neglect others needs when I have the means donate my time or money because I would rather help myself and my family." Do not say, "The church only wants to take the money that I have earned. Why should I pay the pastor's salary when he drives a Mercedes, has a big house, and a mega church?" The second statement places you on a conveyor belt named Greed and Envy. It does this by distorting your vision so that its focus is no longer on yourself and what is on the inside of you. Instead, blame is placed on other things so that envy and greed can consume you. As a result, you live to protect what you think there is not enough of, when the reality is that there is an abundance. Do not let someone else's success become a barrier to your peace. **Ephesians 5:5** states this: *"For of this you can be sure: No immoral, impure or greedy person—such a person is an idolater—has any inheritance in the kingdom of Christ and of God" (NIV).*

Therefore, be conscious of who you are, as this is stated in **Revelation 3:15:** *"I know your deeds, that you are neither cold nor hot. I wish you were either one or the other" (NIV).*

However, don't be discouraged because no one is perfect as it is stated in **Romans 3:10:** *"As it is written: "There is no one righteous, not even one" (NIV).* So if you have been singled out by people for homosexuality, not paying tithe, committing adultery, any crime that lead to imprisonment, or drug and alcohol abuse, refer to **Romans 2:1:** *"You, therefore, have no excuse, you who pass judgment on someone else, for at whatever point you judge another, you are condemning yourself, because you who pass judgment do the same things" (NIV).* We must constantly strive to become better and repent daily as we are all flawed. We always will be flawed, which is why constant mindshifts can keep us on the correct path.

Take Action

Taking action is recognizing that you are one small part of a gigantic system. Therefore, understand that you are living life, but your life is not your own. You must live in a way that harmonizes with others for the purpose of a greater good. You must deny the desires of the flesh that do not agree with this statement because it is like this: Imagine yourself on top of a mountain. As far as you can see, there are mountains covered with trees. The sight is beautiful as the blue sky compliments the green trees and the peaks and valleys. Out of all of the trees that can be seen but not counted, is there one tree more significant than the other? Or are they all a part of a bigger system which has a great purpose? Though you are special, you are one surrounded by billions of others, a part of a great system that depends on the next person. What benefit can be named in acting in a way that does not advance the greater system? In this way, **Galatians 5:14** reminds us, *For the entire law is fulfilled in keeping this one command: Love your neighbor as yourself"* (NIV).

Recognize where you are. Are you able to hear the truth, accept it, and apply it to your life? If the answer is no, it is important to become aware of this so you can ask God for His grace and mercy on your life, and in full measure. This is the only thing that can rescue you from the foothold of sinful desires and unawareness. In **John 8:42-47,** Jesus is having a dispute with some religious people and describes the two options we have on earth, which is to be of light or darkness.

If you are of darkness, you do not accept or understand what brings you to light. Although, many who are in the dark wish to come into the light are trapped by their own past acts that have led to repetitive destructiveness of their own life. Recognize where you are, and if you are in darkness, seek God's grace and mercy so you can be saved. **Ephesians 2:4** tells us, *"But God, being rich in mercy, because of His great love with which He loved us, 5 even when we were dead in our transgressions, made us alive together with Christ (by grace you have been saved)"* (NIV). If you seek Him with all your heart, He will rescue you as it is stated in His word. God cannot lie, so feel free to hold Him to His word! You, however, must seek with your heart as said in **Jeremiah 29:13:** *"You will seek Me and find Me when you search for Me with all your heart"* (NIV).

Your ability to decipher your subconscious and conscious thought will come in handy here because this is how you know if you are actually using your heart to seek Him and not your motives. Your motives can also be kept pure with your understanding of greater and lesser abstracts. Now you know not to seek what is lesser because this is the opposite of what you actually desire. **2 Corinthians 4:18** says, *"So we fix our eyes not on what is seen, but on what is unseen, since what is seen is temporary, but what is unseen is eternal"* (NIV). If you know what is actually greater (which is everything God is) you can pursue it. We will no longer be baited to choose what is lesser in place of something greater.

Here is a notable scripture that informs you of how what is lesser will attempt to seem greater in your eyes because it plays to your senses, can be seen through form, and can be attained through you working towards it: **Matthew chapter 13** describes how your faith is killed and cannot allow you to access the kingdom of God on earth. It asserts that faith is the currency of the kingdom of God. You now know what is invisible can only be manipulated by other invisible abstracts. Read this chapter repeatedly until these schemes and tactics no longer work on you.

Defense Mechanism

A major stronghold of wrongdoing is what has been programmed into your memory. This can remind you of actions you are not proud of, how good the things feel that you should not be doing, or even the things that you feel cannot be forgiven. As these thoughts tamper with your will to do good, consider this scripture found in **1 Timothy 1:12-17**. Anything that you can name that you have done cannot amount to what the Apostle Paul did, so if God could use his time in darkness to bring us to the light, the same can be done for you. Therefore, your wrongdoings qualify you highly to express the mercy God has displayed on your behalf. By no means should this encourage you to continue to follow your flesh in satisfying your sensual desires.

So now, seek first the kingdom of God and his righteousness, and you will receive ALL of the things you actually need **(Matthew 6:33).** This is a difficult thing to accept as a defense mechanism because, in order to see the kingdom first, you must believe and have faith that what is unseen is greater than what is seen. Furthermore, to seek his righteousness, you must know the word of God for yourself so that you may see just how righteous he is. But once you have done this, you can have nothing but actually have everything. **Revelation 2:9** states, *"I know your afflictions and your poverty—yet you are rich" (NIV).* Understand how to pray and how to have your prayers answered. This is accomplished by knowing what is eligible to be received by you from the Lord. As stated in **John 14:27,** *"Peace I leave with you; my peace I give you. I do not give to you as the world gives. Do not let your hearts be troubled and do not be afraid" (NIV).*

So what now? Repent, because the kingdom of God is near! **Mark 1:15** says, *"The time has come," he said. "The kingdom of God has come near. Repent and believe the good news" (NIV).* May God bless you along your journey and display his unfailing grace and mercy on your behalf. In Jesus name, amen.

FINAL THOUGHTS

In my final remarks, let me address the sole purpose that I am trying to accomplish. I want you to challenge your thoughts and beliefs towards the life you live and the systems that you believe to be true. Truth does not compromise, and those who know the truth are not swayed by persuasive words that often surpasses one's intellect.

From the information that has been presented to you in this book, you now have the obligation to yourself to pursue knowledge rigorously. You owe it to yourself to question everything you have been taught until you find what you would give even your eyesight or ability to hear for. So, pursue knowledge by reading and mind growth activities until you discover truth. The greater self will know when truth is found as it is not easy to accept or for the body to receive. Remember, when truth is discovered, you would give your eyesight in order to keep it. You would even give your life to represent the truth with fidelity. This is how valuable truth is.

How will you know if you have grown or evolved? You will not take anyone else's word for truth; instead, you will discover it for yourself. One must experience truth for themselves, or else they will always be subject to persuasion. You have been given a formula to understanding truth, which will allow you to realize your identity and fulfill your life's purpose.

If this book has grown your mind, you can find three other mediums to connect with me for more content: audio book, interviews on YouTube, my website, and the music album inspired by the book. These mediums are all located on my website, www.ladrewmurrell.com and on all streaming networks. I can also be searched by name to be connected with on Instagram. You can keep up with the latest posts on Mindshift Mondays.

I will be pursuing many public speaking opportunities that are going to be listed on my website. If you are interested in following this way of thought, take ownership of your own life so that your words, actions, and beliefs match and impact the lives of those around you. This is the greatest service that we can provide one another with.

Look forward to the curriculum for this book to come in the fall of 2019! This curriculum is being created to aid you in taking action. It coaches you step by step, day by day with a predictable formula that will produce the life that was meant for you. This curriculum is filled with actionable steps that, in time, will shift the trajectory of your life towards higher heights. Further details to come through my website about the arrival of this one-of-a-kind curriculum!

I am wanting to ensure that I have made myself clear. Do not take my word for anything. Pick up the Bible and read it for yourself from start to finish and find truth on your own time. This is the only way that you can receive it and believe it. If you agree with me, it is because you already know the truth. If you do not agree with the philosophy presented to you here, it is because you are still searching for the truth.

Everyone, regardless of what they claim or believe, is searching for the exact same thing. That is truth. What we are in pursuit of drives us and connects us to others as well as things. Upon coming to earth, I say there are two things that you do not want to get while you are here: a divorce or a religion. Religion is the opposite of what was taught by the Son of the Most High. The late Dr. Myles Munroe has been my mentor on understanding the kingdom and its impact on earth. The church is your body, and a place of gathering is extremely beneficial. I attend a local church here in my hometown. As divorce rates increase, the more obvious statistic seems to be lack of identity. People do not know who they are or who they are marrying, and consequence to this is divorce or babies out of wedlock.

I recommend limiting the influence that you allow other reading material to have as you formulate a new understanding of the word of God. As I wrote this book, I was not influenced by the writings of any other authors, outside of the Bible. This kept all of my ideas original and current. With that being said, all producers come to be under the same laws and understanding. This book will be similar to others because of that. The more you read the Bible, the more you will notice biblical principles in all meaningful written content.

After I completed this work, I began reading books other than the Bible again. I would recommend the following books to read as these led me to the Bible: The Seat of the Soul by Gary Zukav, *New Earth* by Eckhart Tolle, and *The Essence of Buddhism* by Jo Durden-Smith would be at the top of my list. After my writing was complete, the most beneficial book I've read is most definitely *The Compound Effect* by Darren Hardy.

Either way, consume things that contribute to the mind growth cycle until you become a producer of things that grow your mind and the mind of others. Books are always good to buy, but be selective in what is bought. You do not want to waste time on material that could have been avoided by using the good-better-best thinking system.

I look forward to experiencing the many benefits of the things you are creating!

ABOUT THE AUTHOR

During the time that this book was written, I was hired by a company called Southwind as an executive business coach. This job opportunity came out of nowhere as I was not in the hunt for new employment. I enjoyed being a middle school physical education teacher and coach at the varsity level. My oldest son attended the school that I taught at; I even had him in class during the time that I took the position at Southwind.

I was well aware that I was living the findings of this book in real time, but I did not anticipate such an abrupt interruption to my life. However, the pay increase and personal development the position would allow me was not something I could pass up. Those around me began to listen to my words as my life headed down the path I was teaching right in front of their eyes.

I asked the CEO of the company, Josh Herron, why he called me in to offer me the position. My former football teammate, whom I hadn't spoken with in over a decade, did not hesitate to shoot it to me straight. He told me, "I know you don't have a lot of business experience. That's not why I brought you in. You're a deep thinker, and you know how to get the best out of yourself and others. That's what this company needs." I reiterated my question, "But what made you call me?" Josh's reply stunned me. He said, "For some reason, the universe kept bringing you to the front of my mind, so I listened. I ignored the "qualified" applicants and called you." Long story short, the universe is working with me and not against me! The solution versus victim mindset wins.

My relationship with my sons flourished under this new understanding. They clearly pinpoint the difference between my lesser and greater self. The acts of the lesser are seen for their destructiveness, and we collaboratively explore solutions to not falling victim to environment or circumstance. This book opened up a new door of patience for me as I parent and co-parent. I am always in control of what I can control, and most of the time, it is myself.

I have learned to step outside of myself and evaluate everything under the good-better-best lens and choose from that list how I should proceed. This has had nothing short of a positive impact on my marriage. My next projects will include public education reform, opening a school, and opening a place of gathering where the message of the kingdom will be taught so that life will be lived to the fullness of measure.

CONNECT WITH LADREW MURRELL

Website: www.ladrewmurrell.com
Facebook: LaDrew Murrell
Instagram: @ladrewmurrell
Twitter: A Powerful Mindshift
LinkedIn: LaDrew Murrell

A Powerful Mindshift

www.ingramcontent.com/pod-product-compliance
Lightning Source LLC
Chambersburg PA
CBHW030308080526
44584CB00012B/487